MW01681348

For every copy of From River Bottoms to Rock Bottom and Back sold, $1.00 goes to support the Boise Rescue Mission's Veterans Ministry Program and their continuing work with veterans from across the USA.

BOISE RESCUE MISSION
MINISTRIES

From River Bottoms to Rock Bottom and Back

A Veteran's Memoir of Addiction, Accountability, and Redemption

BY DON LINEBERRY

This is a work of nonfiction. The events and experiences described in this memoir are presented to the best of the author's recollection. Some names and identifying details have been changed to protect the privacy of individuals.

For every book sold, $1.00 goes to support the Boise Rescue Mission's Veterans Ministry Program and their continuing work with veterans from across the USA.

For information, contact:
Don Lineberry
donaldlineberry01@gmail.com

979-8-9959459-0-1 (Paperback ISBN)
979-8-9959459-2-5 (Hardcover ISBN)
979-8-9959459-1-8 (Ebook ISBN)

PRAISE FOR
From River Bottoms to Rock Bottom and Back

"I've had the privilege of knowing Don not only as a colleague in the veteran community but as a man whose life stands as proof that redemption is real. . . . *From River Bottoms to Rock Bottom and Back* is an honest, unflinching account of one veteran's fall and rise again. More importantly, it is a reminder to every struggling veteran that a new chapter is always possible."

—Mitzi Cheldelin, Veterans Outreach & Community Support Director, IDVS

"I didn't see the hardest parts of Don's story—only the man he showed up as once he'd fought his way through them. . . . He never did any of it for recognition—he just showed up, ready to help, every single time. His story is real, unfiltered, and an inspiration to those who are blessed to be a part of his journey."

—Jo Ann Daron, Volunteer Services Coordinator, IDVS

"Don Lineberry has been an instrumental part of my recovery since meeting him in January of 2024 at the Boise Rescue Mission . . . In addition to mentorship, Don has offered spiritual guidance and post-VTC support as I transition back into my community here in Boise, Idaho."

—Chris Perales, MMCS (SW), U.S. Navy

"*From River Bottoms to Rock Bottom and Back* is a powerful story of redemption and resilience. Army veteran Don Lineberry shares his journey from drug and alcohol addiction to recovery, offering an honest look at the struggles he faced. . . . His experience highlights the vital role faith-based organizations play in the overall health of a community—providing hope, structure, and belonging. Today, Lineberry is devoted to helping others overcome addiction, making this an inspiring read for anyone seeking hope and transformation."

—Bill Gardiner, Colonel, M.A.A.L,
Director, Idaho State Police

"Having known Don for over 35 years, this is a revealing and honest depiction of his struggle to overcome addiction, with all the pitfalls that came with it, and still get his life back. Raw and real, it shows how one broken man can rebuild with faith while lifting others, specifically veterans, along the way."

—Steve Woodall, Command Sergeant Major,
Idaho Army National Guard (Retired)

"I've known Don for over a decade, and I've witnessed his journey in a way few others have . . . I've seen the grit, the accountability, and the faith that rebuilt his life step by step. This life story captures that transformation with the same honesty I've seen in him for years. For any veteran or person who feels too far gone, Don's journey is living proof that hope is real and redemption is possible."

—Jacob Lang, Chief Program Officer,
Boise Rescue Mission Ministries

"His story is not unique, but too few people find the road to recovery and the abundant life that can follow sustained effort and a life-altering faith transformation. . . . His care for fellow veterans aligns perfectly with the [American Legion] Riders' ongoing efforts to support veterans across the Treasure Valley. I strongly recommend *From River Bottoms to Rock Bottom and Back: A Veteran's Memoir of Addiction, Accountability, and Redemption*—a real, gripping story that is ultimately uplifting."

—RALPH CAVALIERI, Commander, U.S. Navy (Retired), Commander, American Legion Post 113

"*From River Bottoms to Rock Bottom and Back* would be a great story if it were fiction, but it is not. . . . Anyone who has walked the walk of addiction and recovery will identify with Don, and for those who wonder if they can walk that walk, you'll see that it is true; you can. . . . I pray that Don's story will inspire those addicted to take the walk of faith to sobriety and inspire the sober to reach out with encouragement and support to the addicted."

—REV BILL ROSCOE, President and CEO, Boise Rescue Mission

To every veteran who has ever felt
forgotten or too far gone.
To my sons. You were the reason I kept going, even
when I did not know how.
You stood by me through the darkest nights
and the slowest climbs. Your quiet strength
showed me what family truly means.

To Janet, my partner on "Lucy" and in life.
Thank you for being the one who shared rides
through rain and sun, and for providing the
compassion that encouraged me to stand up and keep
telling my story when shame demanded silence.

And to the brothers still struggling in the shadows:

You are not alone.

Table of Contents

Foreword

I've known Don Lineberry for years—first as a shattered man walking through the doors of the Boise Rescue Mission, then as a reliable, compassionate case manager in our Veterans Ministry Program, helping other broken brothers find their footing. His story isn't dressed up for drama; it's unflinching and utterly real. From army tanks rolling across German fields to jail mats in Twin Falls, from farm illusions in Heyburn to wind therapy on "Lucy" with Janet holding tight behind him.

Don lays bare what far too many veterans endure: the structure of service ends, old habits rush in to fill the void, isolation creeps in, and cracks become canyons. Yet he also maps the improbable road back—a timely Veterans Judicial Outreach intervention, the disciplined grace of the New Life Program, daily choices to stay sober, the rumble of American Legion rides that clear the head like nothing else. This isn't just a memoir. It's a resource wrapped in truth. Hand it to a buddy who may be spiraling: "Read this. It's like my story, but he made it out." Don offers no excuses, no fluff, just hard-won hope without preaching. If you're hurting right now, keep turning these pages. The line is still there. Grab it.

—Leo Hellyer, Boise Rescue Mission Veterans Ministry Director

Preface

I did not set out to write a book. I set out to tell the truth. For most of my life, I carried my story in fragments—some parts I was proud of, many I was not, and others I tried hard to forget. It took years of collapse, recovery, and service before I realized my story had value. Not because it is dramatic or unique, but because it is honest. Because it is lived. Because more people share it than we admit.

This book is not about addiction, the Army, motorcycles, jail, or ministry, though all those things appear on these pages. It is about becoming. It is about the long road from who I was to who I am. It is about the men and women who stood beside me when I could not stand on my own. It is about the mercy that found me in places I never expected to be found.

I wrote this book for the broken, the drifting, the ashamed, the exhausted, and the ones who think they've gone too far to come back. I wrote it for veterans who carry invisible wounds. I wrote it for families who do not know how to help. I wrote it for anyone who needs to hear that collapse is not the end of the story. If my life has taught me anything, it is this: You can rise, not perfectly, not instantly, but steadily.

This book is the record of that rise.

Introduction

The river bottoms of Idaho taught me silence long before the Army taught me noise. I was born in the humid cradle of Mobile, Alabama, in 1957, into a world where faith was as certain as the sunrise and family was the anchor that held everything together. My dad, a Methodist minister, preached grace from the pulpit while living it quietly amid the tensions of the civil rights era—hosting integrated Bible studies, facing late-night threats, and eventually accepting a transfer to Idaho in 1969 to shield his family from escalating danger. We landed in Emmett, where the Payette River wound through orchards and lowlands. Those river bottoms became my first true refuge: fishing alone, watching water carve its patient path, disappearing into nature where no one expected sermons or perfection from me. But life pulls you upstream.

At eighteen, in 1975, I signed on the dotted line for the US Army—delayed entry, a summer pumping gas near West Yellowstone, then Fort Knox, and the rumble of tanks. Germany followed: Kitzinger, the Iron Curtain's shadow, the power of commanding an M60A1 tank, but also the first real cracks—drinking to fit in, hashish that led to an Article 15 and Certified Drug and Alcohol Counseling (CDAC), even brief experiments with heroin that I walked away from before they took hold. I earned a rank of sergeant and honorable discharge in 1978, but readjustment hit hard. The structure vanished; the unrest stayed.

Back in Idaho, the National Guard's 116th Cavalry gave me weekends of purpose—tanks again, crew bonds, diesel, and hydraulics—but my civilian life unraveled. Marriage, a son who became my deepest reason to keep going, trucking jobs, farms, DUIs stacking like unpaid debts. Alcohol led, then meth and opiates followed. A marijuana bust in 1999 stripped away the farm illusion, the second marriage, everything. Homelessness, living in my car at Walmart, blackouts, despair. Finally, on March 7, 2015, DUI in Twin Falls, 197 days in jail, refusing bail until a real recovery path appeared.

That is where grace broke through. A Veterans Affairs (VA) Veterans Justice Outreach (VJO) Specialist reached out to me in that cell and connected me to the Boise Rescue Mission's New Life Program—a year-long, faith-based rebirth of structure, dignity, counseling, work ethics, and spiritual renewal. I graduated in 2016, joined the staff, married Janet—my partner on "Lucy" and in life—in 2021. Today, I serve as Director of the American Legion Riders, volunteer at the Idaho State Veterans Home, and am a case manager for men still in the shadows. Wind therapy on my Harley clears the demons; service to veterans keeps me grounded.

This is not a story of dramatic uniqueness or flawless triumph. It is ordinary in its pain—too many veterans carry invisible wounds that lead to the same edges—and extraordinary in its mercy. The river bottoms gave me silence, the Army gave me noise and power, addiction gave me collapse, and recovery and service gave me purpose. Collapse isn't the end. You can rise—not instantly, but one day at a time.

If you are reading this feeling forgotten, too far gone, or beyond repair, there is a road back, even if it's overgrown and rough. My journey from those quiet river bottoms to my bottom and back is proof. The pages ahead trace every curve, every fall, every hand that pulled me up. Not to glorify the darkness, but to light the way for anyone still walking in it. You are not alone. The rise is coming.

Chapter 1

Rock Bottom

March 7, 2015. Twin Falls, Idaho. The Walmart parking lot never closed, not really. The big blue sign glowed all night like a cold moon, throwing sickly light across rows of empty spaces and the occasional idling semi. I'd claimed the same spot for weeks—far corner, back row, near the cart corral so I could pretend I was waiting for someone. The engine turned off. Windows cracked an inch to keep the glass from fogging completely. The interior reeked of stale vodka, old fast-food wrappers crusted with dried ketchup, unwashed clothes, and the sour metallic tang of my own sweat. A half-gallon plastic jug of cheap vodka sat on the passenger seat like an old battle buddy who'd never leave. It was emptied to the last third now, amber liquid sloshing softly whenever I shifted.

I didn't drink it fast anymore. I sipped. Slow. Deliberate. Each pull burned going down, then spread a dull warmth that pushed the cold back an inch or two. The warmth never lasted. It faded into numbness, the same numbness I'd been chasing since Germany, since the raid, since every promise I'd broken to my sons. That night, the numbness felt final. I no longer cared whether I woke up the next day. More than once in the previous month, I'd sat here in the dark and quietly wondered why I kept waking up at all.

The meth and opiates had already done their worst—brutal highs followed by crashes that left me shaking and hollow. But vodka was constant. Reliable. It dulled the edges enough to sleep, or at least to black out. I leaned my head against the cracked vinyl seat, eyes half-closed, watching the dashboard lights dim and brighten with each passing car on the highway beyond the parking lot.

My mind drifted the way it always did when the bottle took over.

I thought about my sons. How their faces used to light up when I walked through the door, their small arms reaching, voices calling "Dad!" Now those same faces dimmed when I showed up reeking or didn't show up at all. The youngest one still sometimes asked why Dad smelled funny and why Dad was always tired.

I'd lied every time. "Just work, buddy. Just tired."

His small hand used to curl around my finger when he was a baby. Now, I couldn't even look him in the eye without shame twisting in my gut like a knife.

I thought about my parents. Mom's deepening worry lines, the way her voice softened when she asked if I was okay. Dad's quiet disappointment that never turned to anger but cut deeper because of it. The man who had stood for justice in Alabama, who had moved us to Idaho to shield his family from threats, who was now having his middle son disappear into a bottle in a Walmart parking lot. I could still hear his sermons on grace and the path home to God. Grace felt like a word from another life.

I thought about many things. The people I had hurt. The wives who had believed my promises. The jobs I had lost. The farm illusion shattered in 1999. The kid I once was, who started grounded in river bottoms, watching bobbers dance on the Payette, and somehow ended up here, parked under fluorescent lights, wondering if the next drink would be his last.

The worry was real and thick, a physical weight in my chest no alcohol could lift. It pressed down, familiar and heavy, whispering that I was beyond saving. That this was simply who I had become. Part of me believed it. Another part wanted to believe it—because believing anything else meant I had to do the work I was terrified to start.

I lifted the jug again for one more pull. The burn was sharper now, almost angry. I set it back on the seat and stared at the floorboard. Scattered empty wrappers. A crumpled receipt from the previous week's visit to the gas station. A child's drawing I'd kept from years ago of stick-figure me holding hands with stick-figure boys. I picked up the keepsake and smoothed it against my thigh. The crayon lines were blurred. I wiped my eyes with the back of my hand and let the paper fall.

Headlights swept across the windshield. I didn't flinch. It was just another car cutting through the lot. Then red-and-blue lights ignited, strobing through the glass like an accusation. My heartbeat surged hard, once, then settled into a dull thudding.

Car doors slammed shut. Boots hit asphalt. A voice, sharp and professional, said, "Sir, step out of the vehicle."

I sat frozen for a second. The jug of vodka stared back at me. I reached over, capped it slowly, and set it on the floor as if it mattered. Then I opened the door and stepped out into the cold. The clean air hit me like a sharp slap, nothing like the stink inside the car.

Two officers approached, their flashlights cutting

across my face, my hands, and the open door.

"Hands where we can see them."

I raised them slowly.

They clicked cuffs on, their cold metal biting my skin. They patted me down, finding nothing but lint and shame. One officer shone his light inside on the half-gallon, the wrappers, and the child's drawing on the seat. He didn't comment. Just read me my rights in a flat voice while the red-and-blue lights strobed the parking lot in pulsing color.

The ride to jail was almost silent. Radio crackle and my own ragged breathing. Streetlights slid past like memories I couldn't hold onto. I stared out the window at the dark shapes of buildings and wondered if this was finally the end I'd been circling for decades.

Twin Falls County Jail smelled of bleach and despair. Fluorescent lights buzzed overhead, never off. The constant clank of doors locking filled the air like a heartbeat, along with echoing shouts from other cells through metal bars. Intake was mechanical with fingerprints and a mugshot. They took my shoes, my belt, my dignity. I stood barefoot on cold tile while they inventoried what little I had left. The orange jumpsuit hung loose on my frame.

The cell block door slid open with a hydraulic hiss. There were thin mats on concrete floors. Graffiti names, dates, and curses scratched into the walls. I was led to a lower bunk near the back. The mattress smelled of sweat and bleach. I sat on the edge, elbows on knees, staring at the floor. The hallway light cut a thin yellow line across the concrete, unbroken except where shadows from the bars fell. I watched that line for hours.

Cellmates came and went, some loud, some silent. Stories drifted through the bars at night of DUIs, fights, and bad checks. One guy cried quietly after lights out. I didn't.

I just sat. Stared. Asked myself how I'd let it get this far.

The answer was simple and brutal—I'd chosen the bottle over everything else. Over my sons. Over my family. Over myself. I didn't just wake up one morning in that parking lot. The road there had started decades earlier on the banks of those quiet river bottoms where silence first became my teacher, in Germany, where the first cracks appeared. Every choice, every drink, every blackout had led here.

I refused bail. Stubbornly. Stupidly. Waiting until a real recovery path appeared. Days blurred. Court appearances in chains rattled with every step. The judge's voice was stern but not cruel. "You're a stubborn but smart man," Judge Harris said when I refused to walk out until something real showed up. I sat listening, nodding, the weight of restraints heavy on my wrist.

Nights were the worst. The hallway light never changed. I lay on my thin mat, back against the cold wall, watching that thin line of yellow light stretch across the floor. Sometimes I prayed short, wordless supplications my dad would have recognized. Sometimes I just stared. Wondered if the boys still thought about me. I wondered if anyone did.

It was 197 days. Thin mats. Mystery-meat trays. Graffiti walls. Cellmates' echoing crashes. And that hallway light, steady as a promise I didn't yet believe.

Rock bottom isn't dramatic. It's quiet. It's sitting alone in a concrete box, with the smell of bleach and regret, and finally running out of excuses. It's the floor you push against to stand.

That DUI wasn't punishment. It was the intervention I'd dodged since Germany. And somewhere in those 197 days, grace found a crack to slip through.

Buddy Note

March 7, 2015, Twin Falls Walmart parking lot. Living in the car with cracked windows, the stale smell of vodka, fast-food wrappers, unwashed clothes, and an empty half-gallon that was like an old battle buddy. Blood alcohol content (BAC) was way over. Cold cuffs on. Radio crackled alongside ragged breathing. Locked up for 197 days and refused bail. Stubborn fear mixed with faint hope for a real path. Bleach and despair smell. Thin mats, mystery-meat trays, graffiti walls, cellmates' stories. Nights staring at the hallway light on the floor, asking how I let it get that far. Brutal answer—I chose the bottle over sons, family, and self.

Rock bottom is the floor you push against to stand. That DUI was the intervention I dodged since Germany. Judge Harris said I was "stubborn but smart." Stubborn kept me breathing until VJO threw the New Life Program rope. One conversation, one application, one ride to Boise with clean air after months of stink. If you're on that mat tonight—or still in the car saying "tomorrow"—you're not too far gone. Shame feels permanent because it's held the mic too long. At booking or court, say six words: "I'm a veteran—please flag VJO." Those words can bring real help instead of another cycle. Call 988 (press 1) for a local Veterans Center, a sober Legion veteran, or Boise Rescue Mission at (208) 343-2389 if in Idaho. Hold one more night. Tell someone you served. The discipline from basic training and motor pool can carry you through. Take one honest reach out. The rise is closer than it feels.

PART I

Roots

CHAPTER 2

STEADY GROUND SHAKEN

April 21, 1957. Mobile, Alabama. I entered the world as the second of four children inside a modest white-frame parsonage that shared a narrow yard with the Methodist church where my father preached. The house breathed calm certainty with the crisp scent of starched laundry drying on the line, Sunday pot roast simmering with rosemary and onion, the faint musty sweetness of old hymnals stacked on the parlor shelf. Life moved in predictable orbits of morning devotions, evening prayers, the soft creak of floorboards under stocking feet. There were no raised

voices ricocheting off the walls, no amber bottles hidden behind the flour tin, no half-heard adult whispers about an uncle who "couldn't stop." The word *addiction* simply did not exist in our vocabulary.

Dad was up before first light. The percolator hissed on the stove while he sat at the scarred oak table, Bible open, pencil scratching sermon notes in the margin. Golden lamplight illuminated the pages as he wrestled with grace, forgiveness, and the long road home to God. Mom flowed through the house like a gentle tide, kneading biscuit dough with strong, floured hands, mending torn knees on school trousers, correcting us with a quiet word or a single arched brow that carried more authority than any shout. Discipline arrived wrapped in love, and correction never felt like punishment.

Sundays held the week's center of gravity. We lined up on the porch with starched white shirts, polished shoes, hair still damp from combs, and walked the short gravel path to the church sanctuary. Inside was polished oak and a worn red carpet. The air was warm with the wheezy sigh of the old pipe organ. Hymns rose like a tide with "Amazing Grace" rolling deep and slow, "How Great Thou Art" lifting toward the rafters until the rafters themselves seemed to vibrate. I perched on the front pew, legs dangling, patent shoes barely brushing the floor, and I watched Dad behind the pulpit. His voice carried steady and measured, each sentence a promise delivered without hurry. When the congregation answered "Amen," the sound wrapped around me like an embrace. We were more than a family in those moments—we were a living illustration of the sermon—every restless shift of my brothers, every stifled yawn from my sister, every quiet glance Mom sent our way reflected on Dad's calling. The weight of that reflection settled on me early, soft but persistent, like damp cotton on skin.

Fishing holes became my first private kingdoms. Dad led us to farm ponds ringed with cattails or down to the slow-moving river a mile from the house. Sun-bleached docks creaked under bare feet with splinters waiting like tiny traps. Dad threaded wriggling nightcrawlers or fresh shrimp onto hooks with the same deliberate care he used opening Scripture, then showed us the flick of the wrist that sent the fishing line arcing clean. We sat shoulder to shoulder, poles propped on forked sticks, water lapping softly below. The tiny red-and-white bobber danced hypnotically—then plunged—the rod bowed, and the line sang through the guides. I cranked hard, forearms burning, until a catfish erupted in a thrash of whiskers and silver scales. Dad's quiet laugh rolled out as the fish slapped the dock. Later, Mom dredged fillets in cornmeal, and the kitchen filled with the sharp sizzle of hot oil and the clean, sweet smell of river fish crisping at the edges.

Those hours on the water schooled me in stillness. Sit. Watch. Feel the subtle tug before you see it. No rush. No clamor. Only wind rustling the overhanging branches and the patient slap of small waves against pilings. As the middle child sandwiched between louder brothers, I learned early that attention was something you earned by not demanding it. Feelings of anger, hurt, and fear were not aired but set aside. When sadness pressed in, Mom would hand me a chore list and say gently, "Count your blessings, Donnie," until the emotion dulled under the rhythm of sweeping or weeding. Dad preached endurance rooted in faith, where talking feelings out was rarely part of the prescription. Pain stayed inside, silent and private.

But the world beyond our parsonage fence was growing

louder and more dangerous. The 1960s South crackled with electricity that no sermon could fully contain. Marchers in Selma faced billy clubs and tear gas. Birmingham's 16th Street Baptist Church exploded, taking four little girls with it. Boycotts, fire hoses, snarling dogs on television, images that seeped into our consciences even when the set was off. Dad refused to stay silent. From the pulpit, he preached "love thy neighbor" without footnotes or exceptions.

After services, certain deacons pulled him into the hallway, faces flushed, voices low and urgent. "Reverend, you're stirring trouble."

His reply never wavered. "The Lord calls us to justice, not comfort."

Those stands carried a price. The phone rang after midnight—shrill, insistent, slicing sleep like glass. Anonymous notes appeared under the front door, scrawled in block letters thick with menace. I woke once to the sound of Dad's footsteps pacing the living room. The receiver was pressed to his ear, his voice low and steady while Mom stood frozen in the hallway, arms wrapped tight around herself. At the dinner table, his shoulders carried a new tension, and conversations were hushed after we were sent to bed. I felt fear without a name for it—the way a child senses a coming storm before the first drop falls. The man who had taught us grace now bore its cost in late-night silences and behind locked doors. Watching him carry that burden carved something permanent inside me of admiration edged with helplessness, love shadowed by the first faint recognition that goodness could invite harm.

The Methodist conference eventually acted. Our 1969 transfer to Idaho was framed as a new assignment, but we understood it differently, as a quiet extraction from a fire that had grown too close. The city of Emmett received us in late summer. After Mobile's suffocating humidity, the dry wind felt like a sharp, almost painful slap. Orchards stood in neat rows across the valley floor as apple trees bent under heavy fruit. The Payette River threaded through the lowlands like a silver vein, cottonwoods flashing silver-green in the breeze. Our new parsonage was smaller, the rooms brighter, the air thick with pine resin and sagebrush.

Dad walked the property that first evening, already sketching flower beds for Mom in the dirt with a stick. Mom unpacked boxes, humming hymns to stitch normalcy back together. My siblings scattered, with older brothers claiming territory and younger ones racing around the yard. I stayed on the porch steps, staring at the massive mountains that rose suddenly to the north. Their scale made me feel small, unmoored, far from everything familiar.

School began a week later. Junior high hallways smelled of floor wax and adolescent sweat. Faces were unfamiliar, accents clipped and flat compared to the slow, molasses-like cadence of home. My lingering Southern drawl of "y'all," "fixing to" drew instant attention, words that landed like foreign coins.

Being the new preacher's kid turned every glance into scrutiny. Eyes followed in the corridors, and whispers hid behind hands. "That's the minister's boy." Some were curious, some testing, but the expectation to behave hung heavy. Excel. Reflect well. Room for error felt razor-thin.

Buddy Note

Many of us grew up in homes that looked rock-solid—church every Sunday, family meals, parents who didn't drink or fight loudly. Mine was one of them. It gave me roots. It gave me patience. It gave me the ability to sit quietly on a riverbank for hours watching a bobber.

Emotions got worked out with chores or prayed away in silence. Pain stayed inside. If your childhood gave structure but left quiet gaps—unspoken hurt, questions nobody asked, the sense you had to be "good" to be loved—those gaps don't disappear when you put on a uniform. They travel with you. They show up in barracks' insomnia, in bottles that promise to fill what words never could.

You don't have to keep carrying that old silence. The discipline that got you through basic can get you through one honest conversation now. Tell someone—VA counselor, Vet Center, sponsor, close friend. Name what stayed buried.

CHAPTER 3

RIVER SANCTUARY

When we arrived in Emmett, I did what I had always done and headed straight for the river. The moment my bike tires left pavement and crunched onto the gravel lane, the knot in my chest loosened. I'd stash my bike under the bridge, the metal frame cool against my palm, then traverse my way downstream. Walking down along the overgrown banks, I stepped into a world that asked nothing of me. The air smelled of wet stone, sun-warmed willow leaves, and the faint mineral smell of river mud. Willows curved overhead like green cathedral arches, their narrow leaves brushing my face with cool, papery touches. Gravel shifted and rolled under my sneakers, each step a small negotiation for balance.

I could hear the river before I saw it, a soft lapping against the rocks, a low gurgle where the current curled around submerged logs, the occasional splash of a fish rising. Dragonflies hovered in shafts of sunlight that pierced the canopy, their wings flashing iridescent blue. The scent of damp earth rose when I dug worms from the soft bank's soil, rich and alive, mixing with the sharp green smell of crushed willow stems when I grabbed branches to steady myself.

The lime-green tackle box I carried, scratched and dented from the long bike ride west, bumped against my leg with a familiar plastic clatter.

Out came the old-timer pocketknife, its bone handle smooth from years of use. I'd select a willow branch, slice it clean, and whittle a sturdy forked stick while the river whispered beside me. Spotting the perfect eddy, where the current slowed into a glassy swirl flecked with foam and fallen leaves, I'd wedge the stick deep between three heavy basalt rocks, pitted and ancient, their surfaces still warm from the sun. I baited the hook with a fat worm that squirmed cool and slick between my fingers, cast, and set. Then I was free to wander for hours, the world narrowing to small wonders.

Muskrats slipped into their holes with soft plops, their wet fur glistening. Deer lifted their heads from gravel bars, their dark eyes meeting mine across the water, their ears flicking before they melted back into the brush. The sun warmed my shoulders through my T-shirt; the rocks chilled my bare feet when I waded. Sometimes I'd lie back on a flat boulder, eyes closed, letting the river's steady voice drown out the echo of Sunday-school expectations and hallway whispers. In those moments, the knot inside me unraveled. No one was watching. No one needed me to be perfect. I could daydream without guilt about trapping muskrats for pocket money, about panning for gold flakes in the shallows the way the old-timers had, about being anyone other than the preacher's boy. The river bottoms didn't judge. They simply held me.

Winter introduced ice fishing with Russell, my first real friend in Idaho, an outsider like me, quiet but steady. We bundled in coats, dragged an auger across the frozen surface, and drilled holes that exhaled cold vapor. One January afternoon, the ice betrayed us. Russell stepped too far, searching for deeper water. A sharp crack sounded—like a rifle shot—then black water swallowed him to his shoulders. I lunged, grabbed his forearm, and pulled with everything I had. The shelf of ice gave under my knees, cold slammed through me like a fist, my lungs seizing. We thrashed, scrambled, clawed onto solid ice, clothes heavy, teeth chattering uncontrollably. Officers in a patrol car found us shivering on the bank, wrapped us in blankets, and drove us home. Mom gasped at the door. Dad dropped to his knees in thanks. Russell and I laughed about it later, voices shaking, but something permanent had shifted in us. The river had shown its beautiful, indifferent, powerful teeth. Respect settled deep.

That first summer as the new kid carried its own kind of ache. A curly-haired blonde girl named Rhonda had moved into town at the same time we did. Both of us were eleven. We met one bright Sunday morning in church. Our parents had quietly arranged it: hers, wanting her to be kind to the minister's son; mine, urging me to show the new girl around. Every Sunday, we sat together on the back pew, sharing hymnals, whispering about nothing important. I started to hope—really hope—that when school started, I'd have a cute girlfriend, someone who saw me as Don, not just the pastor's kid (PK). The daydream felt warm and possible in the quiet of the church's sanctuary, but school shattered it in a single week.

Rhonda stepped into the crowded hallways and was swept straight into the popular circle through laughter, notes passed, and invitations to sit at the right lunch table. I stood on the outside, the new kid with the Southern drawl and the preacher dad. Our Sunday friendship faded into polite nods between classes. *Oh well*, I told myself on the walk home, bike tires humming past over pavement. I still had the river. As a scrawny, Tom-Sawyer-sort-of kid fresh from Alabama, I convinced myself I was content.

But the truth sat heavier.

Being the PK in Emmett wasn't just awkward—it carved something permanent. Every Sunday, I watched Dad preach grace from the pulpit while feeling the invisible weight of living it perfectly at home and at school. If I got a B instead of an A, if I forgot to hold the door for someone, if I laughed too loudly at a joke in the hallways, whispers followed. "That's the minister's boy." The fear of embarrassing him, of embarrassing Mom, of somehow weakening the very faith that had brought us there, pressed down until breathing felt careful. Emotions went underground. Sadness, anger, confusion, I put them away the way Mom had taught me to fold laundry, neat and out of sight. "Count your blessings, Donnie," she'd say with a gentle smile when I looked heavy. So, I did. But the blessings never quite filled the hollow place where a normal boy's feelings were supposed to live.

The river bottoms became the one place those feelings could surface without shame. There, on the gravel banks with the sun on my neck and the current tugging at my ankles, the constant performance finally stopped. I could trip and curse under my breath. I could sit for an hour watching water carve stone and let tears come if they wanted—though they rarely did. The sensory world grounded me with the cool shock of river water when I waded deeper, the gritty texture of wet sand between my toes, the sweet-sharp scent of willow sap on my hands after cutting a new pole, the distant call of a red-winged blackbird cutting through the rustle of leaves. In those long afternoons, something fragile took root inside me—a stubborn little belief that I could survive the watching eyes, the whispered expectations, the quiet fear that I might never be enough. The river didn't fix the knot; it simply let me set it down for a while.

Those junior high years on the Payette shaped me more than I knew. The pressure of PK life taught me early on that feelings were to be managed alone, that belonging came with conditions, and that safety could vanish with one wrong glance. The river taught me the opposite—that there were still places where I could simply be. That contrast would follow me for decades, into high school rebellion, Army noise, and the long slide into bottles of alcohol and silence. I didn't understand it then. I only knew that when the school bell rang, and the hallways closed in, the river bottoms waited downstream, steady and forgiving, ready to let a boy breathe again.

Yet even the river couldn't follow me everywhere. The weight I carried into those sunlit hours always waited on the bank when I climbed back on my bike and pedaled home, patient as the current, whispering that the ground beneath me might still shift, and that no sanctuary, however beautiful, could last forever.

Escaping to the river bottoms and mountains to hunt and fish was not just my way of stepping away from the pressures around me—it became the pattern I followed whenever the world felt too heavy. I had been raised around hunting and idolized my grandfather, a real "man's man" back in Alabama. Grandpa Phillips, or "Pawpaw," was a welder in the Mobile shipyards who liked his drink. He kept blue-tick hounds, ran a flat-bottom johnboat with an Evinrude outboard motor for trout lines and night catfishing. Visits to his place "up to the country," that piney part of Alabama with red dirt roads, meant hearing the dogs baying from a mile off. Relatives dotted the hills, all with open wells and outhouses. Grandma Alice sat on the raised porch in wooden chairs seat-bottomed with dried deer hides, a pinch of Skoal tobacco in her cheek, spitting dark streams of it at any rooster that strutted too close.

Pawpaw was my childhood hero. I counted the days until I'd be old enough for the family deer hunts with him and my uncles. Dad told stories of squirrel hunting when Pawpaw would pause, say "Hold on a minute, Bill," duck behind a stump or deadfall, pull out a bottle of clear liquid for a quick sip, then carry on. Yep, Grandpa loved his drink. Always a six-pack of Pabst Blue Ribbon beer in the refrigerator. Between his example and country songs about the long lonesome road and drinking to forget, I started romanticizing booze and escape early. Hank sang it, so I believed it. Running to the woods or to the bottle was just what a man did when troubles closed in.

Later, after the Army, when my world finally steadied, and I settled back in Idaho, I picked up hunting again. No squirrels or coons there, but plenty of pheasants, rabbits, deer, and elk. Just like Pawpaw before me, I loved poking around the woods and mountains, scouting whatever season was open. All year I planned fall hunts, talking at the plant or the sporting-goods store about weather, luck, where the crowds were thickest, how the herds were faring. In my middle years, besides learning to hide my drinking better, I'd become a pretty good hunter who knew the honey holes to fill my tag, avoided weekend packs, and took off alone for a weekend or a week to roam and drink.

I remember one time I'd just turned off a deserted road onto the highway, beer between my legs, a loaded 270 Winchester on the pickup seat beside me. In the rearview, a vehicle closed fast about a mile back. County sheriff. *Shit.* Loaded gun in plain sight, open container. I tried to drive and unload the bolt-action simultaneously. I never quite managed it. Lucky for me, he blew past without stopping. I headed up through Sun Valley, turned west on Warm Springs Road toward the headwaters to hunt elk—and drink, of course—all by myself.

The river bottoms taught me silence and patience when I was young. Hunting gave me the same solitude later, but by then the quietness had me carry a bottle in the pocket, and put a flask behind the seat. What began as refuge slowly turned into something else—escape laced with the very thing I was trying to outrun.

Buddy Note

Many of us had a spot that felt safe when the world watched too hard—riverbanks, tree stands, anywhere the noise quit. For me, it was the Payette with gravel underfoot, willow scent, muskrat plops, deer staring across eddies. No performance. Just breathing. The knot in my chest loosened. I could daydream without shame.

But even the best hideout has limits. What started clean in Alabama—Grandpa Phillips' hounds baying, night catfishing, squirrel hunts with quick sips behind stumps—carried a shadow. Pawpaw was my hero with a drink in hand, country songs selling the lonesome road, and the bottle that went with it. I bought it early. Escaping to the woods (or the drink) became what men do. That pattern followed me from Alabama piney woods to Idaho mountains, from boyhood bobber-watching to solo elk hunts with beer between my legs and a 270 on the seat. Solitude that once healed quietly became hiding.

Rhonda, at eleven years old, still stings with church hope, then hallway rejection. I told myself the river was enough. But the seed was planted, you're not quite enough. It travels to keggers, barracks, farm porches, truck cabs, and Walmart lots.

If you were raised watching—PK, good kid, soldier who had to measure up—the grooves run deep. Pressure teaches burying feelings, seeking places where eyes can't follow. River taught patience, hunting taught escape. Both taught silence. But silence without honesty turns into isolation.

Watch when your sanctuary starts carrying a flask, when scouting becomes more about the bottle than the track. When "just me and the mountains" means "just me and the drink." That's the old pattern talking—same one from Pawpaw's hidden sips—that waits for stress, loneliness, and exhaustion. It whispers you've earned the run. You don't have to let it win.

CHAPTER 4

HIGH SCHOOL YEARS

Blackfoot, Idaho, 1972. The town stretched flat and endless beneath a sky so vast it seemed to press down instead of open up. Potato fields rolled to the horizon like a brown ocean frozen mid-wave, broken only by the Snake River's wide, muscular current. The air tasted of dry earth, freshly cut hay, and the faint metallic tang of irrigation sprinklers hissing in the distance. Compared to the intimate, shadowed bottoms of the Payette back in Emmett, this place felt exposed—raw, windswept, unforgiving—nothing here whispered secrets or offered hiding spots. Everything stood revealed.

I walked into Blackfoot High carrying the same

invisible weights I'd hauled across two previous moves: new kid, PK, the boy whose family had already uprooted twice in three years. The PK label clung to my skin like wet clay. Teachers knew before I even opened my mouth that my father was the new Methodist minister. They called on me first in every class, eyes expectant, voices laced with that quiet assumption of higher standards. "Lineberry, what do you think?" A wrong answer, a slow response, even a simple shrug felt like public failure. Classmates whispered the old nicknames of "Bible boy" and "holy roller" behind cupped hands, some smirking, some merely curious. I hated the spotlight that followed me down every hallway, hated how a laugh too loud or a joke too sharp could draw the verdict of "Didn't think preachers' kids did that." A single D on a report card landed heavier than any stone in my chest. The pressure was never spoken aloud, yet it coiled tight around my ribs, squeezing tighter with every passing week.

I carried it home, too. At the dinner table, Dad would ask about my day, voice gentle but eyes searching, the same eyes that had faced down threats in Alabama. Mom's quiet smile held the same unspoken question of, *Are you reflecting well on the calling?* I smiled back, nodded, and changed the subject to the weather or the latest weather report. Inside, a low dread simmered, fear that one slip could tarnish everything they had sacrificed to protect us. Feelings for them warred with the confusion of being watched so closely; I wanted to shield them from any shadow I might cast, yet I felt myself fracturing under the gaze.

Hobbies became my fragile escape routes, brief pockets of peace amid the constant surveillance. Fall hunting with my .22 carried me out into the sagebrush hills at dawn, boots crunching frost that glittered like shattered glass.

The sharp bite of cold air stung my lungs. Gun oil smelled clean and metallic on my hands. The crack of the gunshot split the silence, sharp and final, followed by the soft weight of a rabbit, warm, still, a small life ended by my choice dropping into my game pouch. In those moments, a strange reverence washed over me at the precision and the cost. Yet even there, the old dread lingered of what if someone saw the preacher's son with a rifle and blood on his hands?

Fishing the Snake's swirling eddies taught patience all over again. I stood knee-deep in the cold rush, reading the current's hidden seams, watching trout rise with silver flashes. The line whispered through the air, delicate as breath. When a fish struck bait, the rod bent alive in my grip, heart leaping with sudden wild joy. For those suspended seconds, the world narrowed to water, line, and fight—freedom pure and fierce. Floating on inner tubes with a handful of friends offered something closer to pure release, sun baking bare shoulders, rubber warm and slick against skin, water lapping in lazy rhythms, while laughter bounced off canyon walls. We drifted for hours, the current carrying us downstream, the sky an endless blue bowl above. In those golden stretches, a fierce love swelled for the fragile normalcy we'd carved—friends who didn't know the PK weight, moments when I could simply be a boy, not a symbol.

But the jobs I took on alongside school grounded me in harsher realities. Restaurant janitor after closing, mopping greasy floors under harsh fluorescent glare, bleach burning my nostrils, fryer oil thick and rancid in the air. Dishwasher in the steaming back room, scalding water turning hands raw and red, clatter of plates like distant artillery. Driving the catering truck to weekend events brought brief road freedom, an engine rumbling beneath me, wind whipping through the open window, the taste of dust and possibility. Potato harvest in the fields was pure endurance with dust choking my throat, my back screaming under heavy sacks, and sweat carving clean tracks through grime. Each paycheck, thin as they were, felt like proof I could stand on my own two feet. I spent them on fishing lures, bicycle tires, and gas for stolen hours of escape. Yet every dollar earned carried an undercurrent of restlessness, a low hum I could not silence, that *This is not enough, this will never be enough.*

By senior year, the restlessness had become a constant roar in my blood. Graduation in 1975 arrived with a D average and a cap tossed high into the air—relief and panic colliding in my chest. No plan. No clear path. The future yawned like those endless potato fields, flat and intimidating. Then an Army recruiter appeared at school assemblies, posters blazing with adventure, crisp uniforms, and tanks thundering across foreign soil. BE ALL YOU CAN BE. The slogan landed like a lifeline thrown into churning water. Structure. Travel. Purpose bigger than my own drift. Tanks of steel, power, and command. I signed the delayed-entry papers for August, heart hammering with a storm of emotions: sharp relief at finally having direction, cold fear of the unknown, aching sadness at leaving home after all the moves my parents had endured for the church, quiet pride that I might finally do something real. Beneath it all, a trembling hope that the Army could quiet the questions, the restlessness, the nagging voice that whispered I was still just the kid who never quite fit in.

High school parties became my secret proving grounds, small rebellions that tasted of both thrill and terror. First sips of beer turned into longer pulls, laughter growing louder, a fleeting sense of belonging sharper than any fishing haul. Cigarettes at first made me cough violently, then I felt cool and defiant between my fingers. The internal war raged constantly and viciously. *This is wrong. This betrays everything. Yet it feels alive, mine, free.* Every late-night evasion, hiding from headlights on back roads, heart slamming against ribs, left me lying awake afterward, pulse racing, promising myself it was the last time. The pull, though, proved stronger than any promise. I was testing edges, testing who I could become when no one from the parsonage was watching. The rebellion looked mild on paper, but inside it felt enormous, a seismic crack widening beneath the surface of the good-son mask I still wore.

The recruiter's office became my private sanctuary. Posters of exotic lands and gleaming tanks stared down. The sergeant's handshake was iron, his voice steady with certainty. I sat there trembling, pen hovering, then signed. The paper felt heavier than it should have—commitment sealed, future claimed.

The Army loomed on the horizon like both anchor and gathering storm. I craved the structure it promised. I feared freedom would strip it away. I hoped it would finally make Dad proud. I dreaded it might break the fragile parts of me, already straining. In the end, I signed because I had to move, had to prove something—to myself, to the watching world, and to the quiet voice inside that insisted I had drifted far too long already.

Buddy Note

Another town, another school, same PK label sticking like wet clay, teachers watching closer, classmates whispering the old names. Pressure sat heavily. Every slip felt like it reflected on Dad, on the calling, on the family. Hobbies and the Snake River gave breathing room, hunting sagebrush hills at dawn, floating inner tubes with friends, carrying away the noise. Those escapes built quiet strength, but first cigarettes behind the barn and beers at keggers felt like claiming something finally mine. Rebellion started small with a bitter first drag and cold first sip, but guilt hit fast and hard. Listen to that, it's louder than later. Jobs proved I could stand alone, but restlessness hummed underneath.

The Army recruiter's promise of structure landed like an anchor in drifting water. If high school feels like shifting sand and edges are fraying, grab grounding things—work, water, honest talk—before drift turns to habit.

You can break the pattern early. Reach out, name it, rebuild before the road forks harder.

Chapter 5

On My Own

That final summer, before the Army swallowed everything, unfolded fifty miles west of West Yellowstone, Montana, in a narrow valley carved by the Madison River. "Sturdy Ville" gas station crouched beside the highway like a weathered sentry, with two red pumps out front, a lunch counter inside smelling of frying onions and strong coffee, a giant wooden propeller bolted above the door as though the place had once been claimed by the sky itself. The owner, Sturdy, an old WWII fighter pilot with a face carved from granite and eyes that had seen too many dogfights, ran the outpost with quiet ferocity. He spoke little and watched everything. The air around the station carried the smell of gasoline fumes and pine sap baking in the sun, and the constant low roar of the Madison rushing cold and clear just beyond the willows.

I arrived in late May 1975, eighteen and restless, still tasting the ink of the delayed-entry papers I'd signed back in Blackfoot, duffel slung over one shoulder. The mountains rose suddenly and massively on three sides, jagged peaks, cutting blue sky like broken glass, while the river carved its patient path below. After the flat, exposed potato fields of home, that place felt vast, isolating, almost holy in its indifference. Freedom, yes—but the kind that could swallow you whole if you weren't careful.

Days snapped into rhythm fast. Open at dawn. Wipe down pumps slick with morning dew, brew a fresh pot of coffee so strong it could strip paint, the percolator gurgling like distant thunder. Early tourists rolled in. Fishermen in battered vests asking about hatches, truckers needing oil checked, and families in station wagons wanting directions to Old Faithful. I learned their language quickly. "Try a Royal Wulff or Elk Hair Caddis today—the fish are looking up." Dipsticks came back black and gleaming. Windshields smeared with bugs got wiped clean. Sometimes I talked the owner of a sputtering RV into a quick carb adjustment, turning the air screw half a turn, watching the idle smooth out, and pocketing a twenty with a nod. Sturdy watched from the doorway, arms crossed, offering nothing but the faintest lift of one brow when the job was done right.

Afternoons quieted after the tourist rush. I restocked the fly rack, cleaned rods in the back room, and listened to the highway hum toward the park entrance. My evenings belonged to the river. I'd grab my fly rod, walk the willow-choked banks as twilight bled purple across the water, and cast into the last gold light, line whispering through the air, leader turning over soft, fly settling with the lightest kiss. Trout rose in slow rings, plopping up softly. The current tugged at my waders like a patient hand. Sometimes I fished alone, sometimes with the neighboring rancher who knew every bend and riffle. Sunsets painted the peaks in fire and shadow. Pine-scented air turned crisp as the stars came out. No crowds. No expectations. Just the rhythm of casting and the long, clean breaths of mountain evening. For the first time in years, the restlessness inside me eased—not gone, but hushed, like a river finding deeper water.

Sturdy held a liquor license and kept four bottles under the counter for the local ranchers who drifted in after dark. They leaned on the scarred wood, talking about cattle prices or drought in low voices, and Sturdy poured shots into chipped coffee mugs without ceremony. When they invited me to join, I accepted those small pours, part of the quiet camaraderie. The whiskey spread warmth through my chest like an old coat pulled on against the cooling night. Never to the point of blackout. Never more than two. Just enough to feel included, to belong for a moment in a place that asked nothing of my past.

Then romance slipped in, soft and unexpected. A college girl, two years older, studying biology, worked the summer as a Fish and Game creel checker. She hiked trails, stopped at river access points, talked to anglers, and recorded catches with a clipboard and an easy smile. We crossed paths one evening at a pull-off beside the Madison. I was rigging my fly rod. She was checking stringers. The conversation started simply. No rush, no performance. She listened in a way that made the air feel lighter. Over weeks, it deepened into something rare and bright, with late-night talks by a campfire behind the station, flames popping, river murmuring in the dark. We dreamed aloud about homesteading in Canada. "Two thousand dollars and yearly improvements could claim a hundred acres," she said, eyes bright with possibility. We pictured a cabin, a woodstove, and land we could work together after my enlistment, after her degree in Idaho Falls. The dreams felt real in the firelight—clean, hopeful, untouched by the shadows I already carried.

The Friday night before, I had to catch the Greyhound back to Blackfoot, so we drove into West Yellowstone for a few beers among the tourists. On the return, we pulled over beside the Madison under a full moon. Elk crossed the river in silhouette, water silver around their legs. We stepped out, stood close, watched the moon shatter on the current. Then we kissed slowly, certain, the kind of kiss that knows time is running out. We held each other for a long moment, neither saying goodbye, just breathing in the cold night air and the scent of wet willows. She whispered over my shoulder, "Keep dreaming." I promised I would.

I never saw her again after I dropped her off. No letters arrived. No calls. Life rushed forward, basic training waiting, then structure slamming down like steel hatches. But those months at the Madison remain a bright, unbroken stretch of pine sap on my hands, fly line whispering at dusk, her laugh rising over crackling wood, dreams of a cabin we never built. Sweet. Innocent. Gone too soon.

That summer felt like a gift I hadn't earned. Daily chores at Sturdy Ville kept my hands busy, and my mind occupied. Mountain air cooled the nervous heat that had followed me from Idaho. The river's constant rush drowned the low hum of restlessness. Occasional whiskey with ranchers felt earned, not stolen. The romance—light, real, full of clean possibilities—proved I could still feel hope without reaching for something to numb it.

Yet beneath the calm, a quiet dread simmered. I knew the Army—Fort Knox, drill sergeants, and the roar of tanks—waited. I feared it would bury the riverbank boy who could sit still for hours watching a bobber dance. I feared the structure I craved would also cage me. Confusion twisted inside me, gratitude for this breather tempered by the certainty that it was temporary. Longing for the dreams I'd shared by the fire, for the peace I'd found casting at twilight made the coming goodbye ache sharper. I wanted to hold onto this version of myself, the one who belonged without apology. But a bus ticket sat folded in my wallet like a life sentence.

When I stepped onto the Greyhound in early August, the valley receded in the rear window, the river glinting one last time, mountains standing sentinel. I pressed my forehead to the cool glass, heart heavy with something close to grief. The summer had been calm. Pumping gas under the big propeller. Coffee strong enough to wake the dead. Fly line whispering. Her laugh over campfire smoke, dreams of Canada spoken aloud without shame. No freight train of addiction had yet arrived. Just pine, hot sun, cool evenings, and the rare, fragile sense that life could be gentle.

I carried that golden stretch with me into basic training like a secret photograph hidden in my pocket. When the noise began—sergeants screaming, boots pounding gravel, steel hatches slamming—I would close my eyes for a second and remember the Madison River at dusk, the way its current tugged patient and sure. It reminded me that hope without chemicals had once been possible. That capacity still lived somewhere beneath the armor I was about to put on.

Buddy Note

That final clean summer before the Army, pumping gas under the big propeller, Madison River running gin-clear, fly line whispering at dusk, college girl's laugh over campfire smoke, dreams of a Canadian cabin and a hundred acres—felt like the world finally gave a breather. No freight train yet. Just pine sap, hot coffee, kind mountain air, a rancher poured under the counter, and a temporary, real connection with someone who saw possibility instead of problems.

Many carry one of those "last good summers"—pre-service, post-hitch, between deployments—when life felt open, hopeful, gentle for a minute. Restlessness quieted. Noise dialed down. Dreams came without a bottle or pipe.

Then basic training slammed the door. Structure hit hard, crew bonds formed in steel, but the quiet part—the riverbank kid watching bobbers—got buried under orders, diesel, and Post Exchange pitchers of beer.

I lost that girl and those Canadian dreams. The cabin never happened. Life turned fast and rough. But the memory proves I was once capable of hope without chemicals. That capacity still lives under the scars.

If you've got a golden stretch buried in your story, don't shove it deeper. Pull it out when the road darkens. Let it remind you that clean air, an easy laugh, and bigger dreams are still in there. The kid casting flies at twilight is alive.

The Army gave noise, crew, purpose—things I needed—but couldn't reach the deeper drift already there. Don't wait for cracks to widen. Name what's under the armor while structure surrounds you to a chaplain, battle buddy, or VA counselor (call 988 and press 1). One honest sentence in the dark keeps the freight train farther.

I lost innocent dreams. Rebuilt hope later. Slower, scarred, real. You can too. Honor the bright spots. There's evidence you're capable of more than numbing out.

The river keeps flowing. So can you. One sober sunrise at a time.

CHAPTER 6

BE ALL YOU CAN BE

The recruiter's office in Blackfoot smelled of stale coffee left too long on the burner, polished leather boots, and the faint, metallic bite of gun oil drifting from the display rifles mounted on the wall. Posters of soldiers in crisp fatigues against desert sunsets, tanks churning dust, the bold red-white-and-blue slogan, BE ALL YOU CAN BE, blazing across each one, covered every inch.

The sergeant behind the desk had a crew cut sharp enough to cut glass and a handshake like iron forged in basic. He leaned forward, elbows planted, eyes locked on mine.

"You're a good fit, son," he said, glancing at my shop-class grades and band schedule clipped to the folder. "Armor needs men who think fast and stay cool under pressure."

I'd walked in dreaming of long-haul trucks, the open road, the solitude, the quiet command of a big rig. But the word "tanker" landed differently. Steel, power, a crew sealed inside fifty-two tons of rolling thunder. At eighteen, fresh from high school and that golden Montana summer still warm in my veins, the promise of structure hit like cool river water on fevered skin. I needed an anchor. The drift inside me had grown too loud.

Signing wasn't clean. Delayed-entry program of commit now, ship later. The papers felt heavier than they should have—thin sheets carrying irreversible weight. My hand trembled just enough to notice as the pen scratched my name. Relief surged first—finally a direction, a mission bigger than my own confusion. Then fear rolled in behind it, cold and tight. *What if I'm not enough?* What if the noise drowned the quiet boy who once sat still watching a bobber dance? Thinking of my parents who'd moved twice to shield us, for the dreams I'd whispered by Montana campfires, made my throat close. I wanted to make them proud. I dreaded breaking their hearts if I failed.

First came the Armed Services Vocational Aptitude Battery (ASVAB) in a dim armory room, pencils scratching, clock ticking like a heartbeat. Math and mechanics clicked from years of wrenching on tractors and fixing irrigation pumps, but verbal sections tripped me, words blurring under fluorescent glare. Nerves knotted my stomach into a fist. What if I scored too low? What if they sent me packing before I even started? Two days later, the results arrived. Decent. Qualified for 11E10, tank crewman. Relief washed through me sharply and suddenly, like stepping out of a storm into sunlight. I could still belong somewhere.

The Military Entrance Processing Station (MEPS) in Boise felt clinical, merciless. I drove down with a knot in my gut, potato fields blurring past, sagebrush whipping by the window. The building smelled of disinfectant and nervous sweat. Long hallways echoed with footsteps. We stripped to underwear in a cold room full of strangers, poked and prodded for results. Height 5'8", weight 135 pounds (lean from orchard ladders and river wading), twenty-twenty eyes, blood drawn into chilled vials that made my arm ache. The doctor listened to my heart-thump-thump and asked about asthma, allergies, and old breaks. None. Then the duck walk of knees bent, waddling like humiliated penguins across tile. Embarrassment burned hot, but we laughed to cover it, our voices thin.

The oath came last. A small windowless room, flags on stands, fluorescent hum overhead. A handful of us stood half-dressed, skin prickling in the chill of an over-air-conditioned room. Bare feet stuck slightly to the floor. The officer, uniform starched, voice flat and practiced, raised his right hand. We mirrored him. My hand shook.

"I, Don Lineberry . . ."

My own name cracked on my tongue—barely audible, swallowed by the dead acoustics.

". . . do solemnly swear . . ."

Each word dropped more heavily than the last. Solemnly. Swear. The syllables felt like stones sinking into deep water.

". . . that I will support and defend the Constitution of the United States . . ."

Palm slick against scalp. The flag behind him rippled from an AC vent; red stripes caught the light like fresh blood.

". . . against all enemies, foreign and domestic . . ."

The room shrank. Other recruits shifted, swallowed, breathed shallow. No one spoke. No one moved except to hold the salute.

". . . so help me God."

The final four words hung. My throat closed. I forced them out, voice thin, almost a whisper. They echoed once in my skull, then settled like lead in my chest.

The officer nodded, small, mechanical. "Congratulations. You are now members of the United States Army."

Hands dropped. Someone exhaled hard. A halfhearted clap landed on a shoulder. I stood frozen, skin cold, heart hammering my ribs, staring at the flag I'd just sworn to die for if ordered. No family there to witness it. No river bottoms to retreat to. Just the echo of my own trembling voice and the sudden, crushing weight of everything I'd given away.

I signed the Department of Defense enlistment form, DD Form 4. Inactive reserves under the Delayed Entry Program (DEP). Delayed entry meant I had until August to report, but the commitment was sealed. I walked out taller, prouder—and terrified in a way I hadn't known I could be.

Back home, the reactions were mixed and cut deep.

Dad nodded once. "Service is honorable, son." But worry flickered in his eyes, the man of peace sending a boy toward war's edge. Mom hugged me tight, tears unspoken, her arms trembling just enough to feel. Siblings teased. But the house felt quieter, the air thicker. The PK label shifted. Now I was the soldier-to-be, leaving after all the moves they'd made for the church. Pride swelled—I was doing something big. But dread coiled tighter—I might never come back the same.

Summer blurred by fast. The West Yellowstone job

faded into memory, and the college girl's laugh and Canada dreams slipped like smoke. Then the call came with a report date set. I packed a small duffel, said goodbyes that stuck in my throat, and got on a plane to Kentucky, stomach churning with every mile.

Fort Knox, August 1975. The bus from the airport rolled in under heavy summer humidity with diesel exhaust, cut grass, and distant gunpowder drifting on the breeze. I stepped off, duffel over my shoulder, weight familiar from years of moving, but destination utterly different. No parsonage porch. No river dock. Just a line of recruits in civilian clothes, all looking lost and determined.

Drill sergeants waited at the edge of the parking lot, hats low, voices sharp as bayonets. "Move it, maggots! Double time to the barracks!"

The heat slammed me like a wall. Sweat soaked my shirt in seconds. The parade ground stretched wide, dusty crushed gravel crunching under boots, rising in clouds when trucks passed. Barracks squatted low in brick-green, windows open, bleach and old sweat drifting out. Inside, bunks stacked tight, footlockers like tombstones. I claimed a lower rack near a window, dropped my bag, and felt the first real jolt. *This is it. No going back.*

That night, lights out, bunks creaking, snores filling the dark, my mind raced with thoughts of Alabama summers thick with honeysuckle, Idaho rivers patient and silver, Dad's late-night pacing after threatening calls, the weight of being watched. Sleep came in fitful snatches. I called it fatigue. It wasn't. The old questions had followed me there, quieter under orders and diesel rumble, but still alive. The Army gave noise, crew, purpose—what I desperately needed—but it couldn't reach the deeper drift already rooted inside.

Buddy Note

Recruiter office, stale coffee, leather, gun oil, "BE ALL YOU CAN BE" posters. Adventure, purpose, paycheck, tanks. Signed delayed entry. ASVAB decent—11E10 tank crewman. MEPS Boise, sterile halls, disinfectant, nervous sweat, duck walk embarrassment, oath in a small room, voice cracking on name, promise heavy as lead. No family witnessing. Walked out taller, prouder, terrified. Fort Knox, August 1975. Bus, diesel, and gunpowder, drill sergeants' "Maggots!" Heat wall, gravel crunch, barracks bleach-sweat. Bunks tight, footlocker tombstones. This is it. Small MEPS room, bare feet on tile, hand raised, voice thin on "so help me God." Irreversible weight settled. Chased structure, crew, purpose, bigger than drift. The recruiter sold adventure; I bought an anchor. For a while, it worked. First "maggots" yell, structure slamming like hatches. Felt solid deck after loose gravel. But noise drowned old questions of Alabama summers, Idaho rivers, PK weight, Dad's threats. Lights out, bunks creaking, my mind raced anyway. Called fatigue. Dreams planting roots.

Don't wait for the first Article 15 punishment or a blackout. Name what's under your armor while there's structure around to a battle buddy, chaplain, or medic. One sentence in the dark keeps the freight train farther. Lean hard into noise, crew, and purpose. Qualify gunnery sharp, earn trust. But deeper drift travels. Showed later in gasthauses, bottles. Not weak but human. Discipline through physical training (PT) protects you under the steel if used early. Talk before the bottle—debrief. The rise starts now, in good days, with honest conversation. I lost years pretending cracks weren't there. You don't have to. Oath still stands. Road back too. Keep a hand on the truth.

CHAPTER 7

"TREAD-HEAD" TANKER

Basic training at Fort Knox began at 0430 the next morning with a bugle slicing the dark like a bayonet. Lights snapped on, harsh and unforgiving. Drill sergeants stormed the bay, boots thundering on tile, voices exploding, "Get up, get up, get up!" Feet hit the cold floor in a frantic scramble. Hearts hammered before eyes fully opened.

We learned to make beds so tight a quarter would bounce with corners razor-sharp, blanket tucked hospital-style, pillow centered with military precision. Mistakes earned push-ups until arms trembled and burned. I dropped for dozens in those first weeks, sweat stinging my eyes, gravel biting my palms, shame and exhaustion warring inside me. Every repetition carved deeper discipline in me, but also fear. What if I couldn't keep up? What if the structure I'd craved crushed me instead?

The M16 became an extension of my body, brought everywhere—in the chow line, the latrine, and even to sleep. Disassemble, clean, reassemble blindfolded in dim barracks light after Taps, fingers fumbling pins and springs until they learned by touch alone. The metallic click of parts locking together turned rhythmic, almost meditative, once the fumbling stopped. Sergeants barked corrections. "Faster, Lineberry! The enemy doesn't wait for the charging handle!" But each cycle built muscle memory and quiet confidence. For the first time since the Montana river at dusk, I felt capable of something precise and real.

Runs stretched endlessly. Up "Misery Hill" and down "Agony," Kentucky slopes so steep they posted barrier gates at both ends. The gravel chewed boot soles, the dust coated our throats and lungs, and a cadence of "Left, left, left-right-left!" rang out. Formation running, sweat stinging eyes, hearts pounding in unison. I learned to breathe through the fire in my legs, keep my head up, and match the man ahead of me. Each mile stripped away softness, leaving raw determination. Yet beneath the burn, a low confusion lingered. The pain felt cleansing, but would it ever quiet the questions that still whispered at night?

Obstacle courses tested something deeper. Barbed wire over low crawls tore elbows and bloodied knees. Rope climbs left palms raw and weeping. Log walls were scaled with nothing but grit and the man behind, shoving.

Kentucky mud clung like regret—heavy, cold, sucking at boots. Every cleared barrier settled a small, fierce victory in my mind. I could endure more than I'd believed.

Weapons qualification on the range felt suddenly real. An M16 kicked hard against the shoulder, a sharp crack split the air, and brass pinged concrete. Targets popped at twenty-five, fifty, and a hundred meters, silhouettes like distant men. After a squeezed trigger, I felt the recoil jolt through my bones and watched the paper shred. Gunpowder hung thick amid hot metal, gun oil, and scorched paper. When I qualified, the sergeant gave one small nod. Small praise, but it landed like sunlight after months of shadow. I'd shot my .22 since boyhood, yet this felt different—weightier, final. For a fleeting moment, pride swelled. I belonged there.

Advanced Individual Training (AIT) shifted us to the tanks. The M60A1, "the dinosaur," squatted massive and olive-drab, a diesel rumble vibrating deep in the bones, steel tracks grinding earth, exhaust and hot metal thick inside the turret. The loader, driver, and gunner roles were drilled hour after hour. We climbed in, hatches clanging shut like coffins sealing. Our world narrowed to gauges, levers, and a periscope's narrow slit. Power surged when the engine roared, fifty-two tons of steel answering my hands. I felt invincible for the first time in my life, like I could finally command something larger than my own drifting thoughts.

Crew dynamics formed fast and tight. Four men sealed in a steel box with the commander up top, gunner (me after weeks of proving), loader to the right, driver in the hull. Turret cramped, barely room to turn, air hot with diesel fumes and sweat, a metallic gunpowder taste on our tongues. Every movement was deliberate, coordinated, or jammed. Commander, Staff Sergeant Ramirez, a wiry Texan, mustache sharp, voice cutting through engine roar over the intercom, teased the loader mercilessly about his girlfriend back home, but commands snapped crisp when it mattered. Loader, Private First Class (PFC) Jenkins from Detroit, built like a linebacker, arms slamming rounds home, sweat dripping, always cracking jokes to cut tension. "If this thing rolls, I'm blaming the driver," he'd grin. Driver, Specialist Kowalski from Chicago, quiet, hands steady on controls, eyes flicking gauges like reading scripture. We trusted him with our lives every lurch forward.

Personalities clashed, then fused. Jenkins and Ramirez traded barbs. Ramirez calling him "city boy," Jenkins firing back about Texas barbecue. But hatches closed, engine started, noise swallowed everything.

Intercom crackled clipped commands: "Driver, move out!" "Gunner, target, eleven o'clock, tank!"

I swung the turret, eyes glued to sight, crosshairs settling. "Identified!"

Loader slammed round home—clang of metal, breech closing with heavy thud. "Up!"

Driver kept it steady, tracks chewing dirt. "Fire!" Round out, recoil slamming us back like a mule kick, smoke curling acrid inside. The cycle became instinct: identify, load, fire, adjust.

Live-fire days left us emerging covered in sweat and grime, faces black with soot, ears ringing, grinning like idiots. We were a crew. Had to be. Love grew fierce and unspoken for these men who trusted me with their lives every time the main gun barked. I would not let them down.

Evenings at the PX became ritual. Pay call brought pitchers of cold beer as a reward. Laughter rose over clinking glasses and home stories traded like currency. I drank to belong, with foam cutting my dust-dry throat, warmth loosening the edges. Never a blackout. Just enough to feel part of something larger. Yet a quiet dread simmered beneath. This belonging felt fragile, conditional. One mistake, one crack, and it could vanish.

Nights in barracks brought the first real unrest. Lights out, bunks creaking, snores filling the dark. Mind raced to Alabama honeysuckle thick in summer air, Idaho rivers patient and silver, Dad's late-night pacing after threatening calls, the weight of being watched. Sleep came in fitful snatches. I called it "training fatigue." It wasn't. Insomnia was already planting roots. I just didn't have a name for it yet.

Graduation, December 1975. Uniform crisp, stripes earned. Ceremony on the parade ground with flags snapping in cold wind, band playing, pride swelling so fiercely it hurt my chest. Family absent due to distance, but the accomplishment stood mine alone. I stood tall, shoulders back. For a moment, I belonged somewhere solid.

The Army gave noise to drown silence, crew to replace loneliness, purpose to quiet drift. Yet the deeper questions followed of Alabama summers, Idaho rivers, the weight of being a PK, and Dad's civil rights struggles. They waited in the dark, patiently as the Madison current, ready to rise when the steel and orders fell quiet.

Buddy Note

Basic and AIT hammer in muscle memory, confidence, and crew trust you didn't even know you were missing. That M60A1 turret swinging smooth under your hands, the hydraulic whine, the solid thud of "Up!" before "Fire!" For the first time, maybe ever, you commanded something bigger than yourself. The steel box became home, and the crew became brothers who trusted you with their lives every time the hatches slammed shut.

Lean into that structure hard, because it shows you what discipline and belonging really feel like.

But watch the quiet nights. Lights out, barracks creaking, guys snoring, and your mind won't shut off. Alabama river bottoms, dad's late-night threats back in Mobile, the weight of being the PK everybody watched, all of it starts drifting back in the dark. I called it training fatigue. It wasn't. Insomnia was already planting roots, but I didn't have a name for it yet.

The Army gave purpose, noise, and a crew that drowned out the silence I used to hide in. But it couldn't reach the deeper unrest that was already there. Don't wait for the cracks to widen into canyons before you name what's underneath the armor. Routines are good—honest talk is better. Find one guy you trust, or a chaplain who won't bullshit you, and say the quiet part out loud: "My head won't stop spinning."

You don't have to wait until the bottle becomes the only thing that quiets the noise. Address the drift while you still have structure around you. The same discipline that gets you through quals and motor stables can protect what's under the steel. You're not weak for feeling it—you're human. Talk about it early. The rise starts with one honest sentence in the dark.

You've got the crew now. Use them.

Chapter 8

Germany

The gray, damp, relentless winter of 1976 in Kitzingen hit like a wet slap across the face. Snow didn't drift down like the ones in Christmas cards; it came in heavy, sloppy clumps that turned the motor pool into a knee-deep slurry of mud, diesel, and regret by noon. I was assigned to the 1st Armored Brigade, 64th Armor, 3rd Infantry Division, called the "Desert Rogues." Our M60A1 tanks, the dinosaurs, squatted under camouflage netting like tired old beasts, their tracks already rusting at the edges from the constant wet.

Every morning started the same. "Reveille," morning

roll call, at 0530, formation in the dark, breath fogging under sodium lights that buzzed like angry hornets. First Sergeant "Top" Jackson, a wiry Alabama E-8 who could make "good morning" sound like a court-martial, called roll, then read the training schedule in that slow, gravelly voice. PT followed, consisting of five miles in boots and fatigues, past the chain-link fence that separated the Kaserne from quiet German farmland. Older women in wool coats walked their dogs and nodded politely, as if twenty American tankers jogging in formation at dawn were the most normal thing in the world.

After chow of greasy eggs, toast that tasted like wet cardboard, and coffee strong enough to strip paint, we hit the motor park. The smell never changed of JP-8 fuel, hydraulic fluid, hot metal, and the faint rubbery odor of wet track pads. My crew and I pulled maintenance, checking road wheels, greasing track pins, and running boresight on the main gun. Hands black, coveralls stiff with grease, the cold metal biting through gloves. I was a strong candidate with a clean record, qualified in the range, and promotable. But something inside had already started to shift.

Evenings were when the real rhythm changed.

After duty, most of us scattered. Some went to the library or gym. Most headed off-post to the gasthauses in town. Beer was cheap, half a liter for two marks, and the locals tolerated us if we didn't break the furniture. The Gasthaus Zur Alten Post became our second home, with dark-wood beams blackened by decades of pipe smoke, long tables scarred with knife marks, a jukebox that bounced between American country and German Schlager. I started going along more. At first, it was just one or two Spaten or Warsteiner beers, nursing them slowly, listening to Ramirez tell stories about Texas girls and bad noncommissioned officers (NCOs). The warmth spread through my chest like an old, familiar coat. For the first time since basic training, I felt like I belonged somewhere. But then the nights started stretching.

One December night, the snow was falling thick outside the frosted windows. Inside, it was warm, smoky, and loud. Someone started a drinking game of quarters and Jägermeister shots. I lost track after the third round. Laughter blurred into noise. A German girl with dark hair and a red scarf sat at the next table and smiled when our eyes met. Her name was Monica, and she worked at the bakery near the gate. We talked in broken German and English, her laugh soft against the roar of the jukebox. For an hour, I felt normal—not a soldier waiting for a war that might never come, just a guy talking to a pretty girl.

The ride back to Kaserne was a blackout.

I woke up on the floor of the dayroom, boots still on, head splitting like someone had parked a tank on my skull. My battle buddy had dragged me in and covered for me at formation. Top Jackson called me into his office at 0800. I stood at parade rest, stomach churning, uniform still smelling like stale beer and cigarette smoke.

"Lineberry, you missed PT, you stink like a brewery, and your eyes look like road maps. This is your warning—one only. Next time it's Article 15."

I swore it wouldn't happen again. It did, of course. Not every weekend, but often enough that the pattern locked in like a track pin. I worked hard all week, blew off steam on Friday and Saturday, woke up Sunday regretting it, and promised Monday it would be the last time. The drinking wasn't dramatic—no bar fights, no waking up in a German jail—but it was becoming daily. It dulled the boredom, the homesickness, the low-grade anxiety of living fifty kilometers from the Iron Curtain. I told myself everybody did it. Most did. For me, it was starting to feel less like recreation and more like medicine.

Then the hashish found me.

The taxi drivers in town had connections for small, fifty-gram foil-wrapped blocks, tightly sealed in plastic and almost odorless. On payday nights, we'd score one or two, slip them into a fatigue pocket, and head back to the barracks or a quiet corner of the motor pool after dark. The first time I tried it, I was in the dayroom after lights out, a couple of us passing a tiny pipe made from a socket and a pen barrel. The smoke was sweet, heavy, and almost spicy. The world softened at the edges. The constant low hum of worry about the border, about the next alert, about the letters from home that never quite said what I wanted them to say—all of it eased. For a few hours, the nightmares that had started creeping in after basic finally shut up. I slept like a dead man.

It became part of the rhythm. Not every night, but enough. A quick hit before bed, the sweet smoke curling against the concrete ceiling, the quiet laughter of guys who understood. We kept it quiet. No one wanted another Article 15. But the cracks were widening.

And then came the heroin.

It was only twice. The first time was in a small apartment above a gasthaus, one of the local girls knew a guy. Someone handed me a tiny foil packet and a strip of tinfoil. "Just chase it," they said. "One hit. You'll see God." I hesitated—a voice in me screamed no—but the beer and hash had already loosened the reins. I held the lighter under the foil, watched the brown powder melt and smoke, and inhaled the acrid vapor. The rush hit like a main-gun round, warm, heavy, every nerve lighting up at once. For maybe ten minutes, the entire world felt perfect. No noise. No weight. Just floating.

The second time was a week later. Same apartment. Same foil. The rush came again, but this time something else came with it—a whisper in the back of my head, saying, *You could do this every night. You could live here.* I sat on the edge of the couch, heart hammering, sweat beading on my forehead even though the room was cold. I looked at the guys around me, eyes half-closed, lost in their own clouds, and something in my gut turned over. This wasn't about belonging. This was disappearing.

I stood up, legs shaky, handed the foil back, and walked out into the freezing German night. Snow crunched under my boots all the way back to Kaserne. I threw up twice in the snowbank outside the gate. That was the last time. I walked away before it took hold. But the memory of that perfect floating stayed with me like a ghost—a door I had almost walked through.

Nights I'd lie in my bunk staring at the ceiling, the M60A1's diesel rumble still vibrating in my bones even though the tank was parked half a mile away. I'd get up, clean the .50 caliber in the motor pool under the floodlights just to keep my hands busy, the rhythmic clink of tools and the hum of ventilation fans, the only things that quieted the noise in my head for a few hours. When the shift ended, I still walked past the club. One beer became four. The cycle held.

Kitzingen wasn't where everything fell apart. It was where the first hairline cracks appeared—small, invisible to anyone watching, but deep enough that pressure over time would split them wide open. I was a good soldier on paper, with clean uniforms, qualification on the range, and promotability to sergeant. But inside, something was shifting. The border stayed quiet, and the Cold War ground on like a slow engine. And I kept telling myself I had it under control—right up until I didn't.

Buddy Note

Wet snow turned the motor pool into soup. M60A1 was under netting. Routine of 0500 formation, PT past farms, grease and JP-8 smell, classes on Soviet gear and Fulda Gap. "No warning. They just come." Evenings in the gasthaus with cheap beer, laughter, Monica's red scarf, and her soft laugh. Then the blackout on the dayroom floor. Top's warning of "One only. Next time, Article 15." Pattern locked in hard.

Hash from the taxi drivers, small foil blocks in a fatigue pocket, sweet smoke in the barracks after lights out, and insomnia finally shutting up for a few hours. Then the heroin—twice, chasing that brown powder on tinfoil, the perfect floating rush—. . .and the whisper that I could live there forever. Walked out into the snow, threw up twice, and never went back. But the memory remained.

Still hit the club. One beer became four. Good on paper—clean uniform, qualified, promotable. Inside, spidering. I told myself it was under control—until it wasn't. If you're there in the barracks, motor pool, or bar after duty, the slips start quietly. Extra pour, blackout laughed off, "never again" with a pounding head. Not blowing steam, but a train building speed. Don't wait for Article 15 or forced mirror. Name it now. Find one straight shooter, a battle buddy, a chaplain, or a medic.

Say it in the dark: "Head won't stop spinning, beer's medicine, that one hit felt too good." One sentence keeps the train farther down the track. Lean into your crew and purpose hard. Qualify sharp, earn trust. Don't let the drift ride—it travels. I showed up later in cabs, flasks, farms, Walmart lots. Not weak but human. Discipline from motor stables and border alerts can protect what's under the steel if you use it early. Talk before the bottle or the pipe becomes your only debrief. The rise starts with one real talk. I lost years pretending the cracks weren't there. You don't have to. Watch yourself like the border. The river flows, and so can you. One sober sunrise at a time. Hold on. Tell someone.

PART II

Collapse

Chapter 9

Bad Idea

Kitzingen, late summer 1976. The barracks smelled of wet wool, diesel fumes that never quite left our coveralls, and the faint, sweet residue of hash smoke someone was always trying and failing to mask with aftershave. Payday had just hit. Cash burned holes in fatigue pockets. The taxi drivers in town knew our faces by now and exactly what we wanted when we slid into the back seat and muttered, "The usual." Small, fifty-gram foil-wrapped blocks sealed tight in plastic, almost odorless. Easy to palm, easier to hide.

It started as idle barracks talk after lights out, in low voices and with cigarette glows flickering like tiny beacons in the dark.

Someone said it first. "Mail it home. Buddies back in the States would pay double. Easy money." Laughter followed, half-joking, half-serious.

Then another voice. "Polaroids taped over it, letter folded around. Post office clerk won't even blink." The idea hung there, seductive in its simplicity. Quick cash. A little thrill. Proof I could still be one of the guys—still belong in a place where belonging felt increasingly fragile.

I should have walked away. The voice inside—the same one that had screamed "no" the first time I chased heroin smoke—spoke clearly and urgently. But the other voice, louder now, whispered back, *Just this once. You've already crossed lines. What's one more?* Confusion twisted in my gut. I wanted the crew's approval the way a drowning man wants air. Brotherly love, for Ramirez, Jenkins, and Kowalski, the men who trusted me with their lives every time the hatches slammed, made me desperate to prove I was still solid, still worthy. Fear coiled tighter at the thought of being left on the outside again, fear that the quiet drift I'd carried from Idaho had already marked me as different.

I did it anyway. I taped the block between two Polaroids, one of the crew grinning beside an M60A1, another at the Kaserne gate under sodium lights. I folded a short letter around it, casual, harmless. I felt my heart thump against my ribs as I walked to the base post office. The clerk, a bored German civilian, stamped the package without looking up. I exhaled once I stepped outside, but the relief lasted only seconds. Dread settled in its place, low, constant, like the rumble of an idling engine you can feel in your teeth.

The shipments continued through the summer, small and careful. Each one sent a fresh jolt of adrenaline through my body, followed by a longer, colder wave of nausea. I told myself it was under control. I told myself no one would notice. I told myself the money, when it came, would prove I was smart, capable, not just another broke GI chasing belonging in a bar.

Then the dogs found one.

Army Post Office (APO) mail screening had tightened. Narcotic detector dogs, sleek German Shepherds with noses sharper than any sergeant's glare, walked the outgoing hampers at Frankfurt and unit post offices. One alerted on my envelope, its nose pressed to the seam. It sat and barked once, sharp and final. The package was pulled, X-rayed, and opened. Hashish confirmed. Turned over to the Criminal Investigation Division (CID).

The notification came the next morning. First Sergeant pulled me aside in the motor pool, voice low. "Report to the battalion commander. Now."

Rain sheeted down outside, soaking my uniform in seconds. My boots echoed on wet cobblestone all the way to HQ. My stomach churned so violently I tasted bile.

The PFC at the front desk smirked. "He's expecting you, Lineberry."

Into the commander's office, with a big desk, campaign flags limp in the damp air, gunnery trophies gleaming under fluorescent tubes, photographs of tanks firing on ranges staring down like silent witnesses.

The lieutenant colonel sat rigid, CID report open before him. "Soldier, you're aware why you're here?"

"Yes, sir."

He read charges in a flat, unhurried voice of possession with intent to distribute, trafficking a controlled substance through military mail, violation of Uniform Code of Military Justice (UCMJ) Article 112a, possibly 134. Each word landed like a hammer blow.

Two MPs escorted me to the stockade. Handcuffs cold against wrists. The cell door clanged shut behind me, followed by a metallic echo that vibrated in my skull.

A week later, Article 15 offered non-judicial punishment. I accepted. No fight. Evidence was ironclad. Punishment was a reduction in rank with one stripe gone, forfeiture of pay for months, extra duty, and mandatory CDAC counseling. Shame hit like a hot, main-gun round, leaving me concussed and hollowed out.

Counseling sessions at the base clinic felt like walking naked into a circle of mirrors. Soldiers sat in folding chairs, some with hash cases like mine, some with booze problems, a few with harder paths. The counselor, calm and direct, didn't let anyone hide. "This isn't just one package. It's the habit."

I talked about high school keggers on Freeze Out Hill, PX pitchers at Knox, Kitzingen gasthauses, barracks pipes after lights out. Admitted to the heroin experiments I'd barely escaped.

The counselor pushed. "What's the endgame?"

I shrugged. "Belonging. Unwinding. Money." The words rang hollow even as I said them. It was the first time I was forced to see the pattern of belonging turning into risk, risk into shame, and shame back into the very things that promised escape.

Extra duty meant scrubbing floors at 0500 while the rest of the company slept, with bleach fumes burning eyes and knees aching on tile, silence broken only by the wet slap of the mop. The crew still had my back with quiet nods in the motor pool. "It'll pass." But trust had thinned.

Confidence wobbled. Eyes that once met mine with easy certainty now flicked away a fraction sooner. The confidence of the brotherhood we'd built in the turret gave way to dread. I had endangered it. I had endangered them.

Article 15 was completed, but counseling dragged on with weekly groups and individual talks. Stories echoed mine: "Started with beer." "Needed to sleep." "Just once." They sounded like every excuse I'd told myself. Rank restored later. Promotion to sergeant came slower than it should have. NATO duties defined us again with Fulda Gap patrols and constant vigilance for Soviet silhouettes across the wire. Mud sucked at the tracks. Rain sheeted off armor. Nights in bunkers, cold and damp, wind howling through slits, distant lights flickering across the border like predator eyes.

Hypervigilance became a habit, every rustle a potential enemy, every drill a reminder of the stakes. Nightmares worsened. Pills from medics chased sleep that never fully arrived. Alcohol blurred edges again as one beer became four. The cycle held.

Kitzingen wasn't where everything shattered. It was where the first deep fracture lines appeared—hairline cracks invisible to anyone watching from outside, but deep enough that time and pressure would split them wide. I was still a good soldier on paper with clean uniforms, range-qualified, promotable. But inside, something fundamental had shifted. The border stayed quiet. The Cold War ground on. And I kept telling myself I had it under control—right up until the moment I knew I wasn't.

Buddy Note

Hashish from taxi drivers. Buddies saying, "Mail it home, easy cash." Taped in Polaroids, APO drop. Dogs alerted Frankfurt. CID traced fast. Busted. Rain walk to the battalion. Lieutenant colonel, stern, charges read. Accepted Article 15 with rank drop, pay forfeiture, extra duty, and mandatory CDAC. Counseling circle with the same excuses, mirroring mine. Naked shame, crew quiet, trust thinned. Completed, rank restored later. Made sergeant, M60A1 gunner. Fulda Gap vigilance, insomnia worse, pills and alcohol blur. Honorable discharge, 1978. Structure gone, cracks widening. It felt like belonging and thrills.

Ended in Article 15 burn with rank and pay lost, floors scrubbed, and CDAC facing my own lies. First real line crossed. Gun loaded. Warning shot. Same voice from keggers to gasthauses to pipes to bottles. Belonging became risk became pattern. Good on paper, spidering inside. If a bad call is looming, don't wait for the next Article 15 or forced mirror. "Just once" waits for tiredness and isolation. Name it now. Find a straight shooter, a battle buddy, a chaplain, or a medic. Say quietly, "I crossed the line, I'm so scared." One sentence slows the train. Lean into your crew and purpose. Don't let the drift ride as it travels to cabs, flasks, farms, and parking lots. Talk before bottle and pipe only debrief. I lost years pretending the cracks weren't there. You don't have to. Watch yourself. You can flow like the river.

Chapter 10

Cracks Appear

The plane touched down in Portland in late 1978 under a sky the color of wet concrete. Civilian clothes hung loose on my frame with no uniform, no orders, no crew to fall in beside. Duffel over one shoulder, the weight felt heavier than any rucksack I'd humped in Germany. The terminal smelled of jet fuel, burnt coffee, and the faint metallic tang of rain-soaked pavement outside. I stepped into the arrival hall and felt the structure I'd leaned on for three years vanish like smoke. No reveille. No motor pool. Just the low hum of strangers moving past and the sudden, hollow

certainty that I had no mission left.

I moved in with my parents temporarily. The parsonage kitchen still carried the comforting scent of Mom's pot roast with rosemary, onion, and slow-cooked beef, and the faint must of hymnals stacked on the shelves beside Dad's open Bible.

They welcomed me with open arms and careful silences. "How was Germany?" Mom asked softly one evening, stirring gravy on the stove.

I gave short answers of good training, solid crew, and cold winters. Never mentioned the hash bust, Article 15, the heroin smoke I'd walked away from twice, or the insomnia that had still woken me staring at barracks ceilings.

Dad nodded. "Service is honorable, son." But worry flickered in his eyes, the same quiet concern that had shadowed him through Alabama threats and Idaho relocations.

I wanted to protect them from the truth. Love surged fierce and helpless. They had already carried enough for me. Confusion twisted deeper. How do you tell the man who preached grace that his son had chased numbness across an ocean?

My first civilian job was prepping semi-trucks on the Sauvie Island docks. Diesel thick in the air, my hands black with grease within minutes, the constant clank of tools and hiss of air brakes. It paid decently. Kept me moving. I enrolled at Portland Community College on the GI Bill, taking trade classes on veteran benefits. I felt direction at first, a faint echo of the purpose I'd tasted in the turret. But the nights pulled harder. A glass of beer after shifts turned into pitchers. Pot from old friends appeared without asking. Occasionally, something stronger, like pills, or a line slipped in like an uninvited guest. Classes slipped. I dropped out after one semester. *Just a break*, I told myself. The lie tasted bitter.

My next job was delivering auto parts across Portland's east side. Van loaded with filters, belts, and spark plugs. I hit garages, chatted with mechanics who smelled of oil and cigarettes. Good tips. Alone time. I started selling small bags of pot to the station guys for extra cash that fed habits I swore were still under control. The neighborhood tavern became routine with a regular stool at the end of the bar, the click of pool balls, neon buzzing overhead, beer after beer until the edges softened. The bartender knew my name. Alcohol filled the Army-shaped hole of no crew, no mission, no orders to drown the questions. Belonging faded—bottles replaced it.

At twenty-three, I tried to root myself. My first marriage lasted two years. We set up house in a small rental with curtains Mom helped hang, and dishes we picked out together. Our son arrived in 1980. Hospital room antiseptic, harsh fluorescent lights overhead, but the moment he was placed in my arms, I felt suspended in time. Tiny, red-faced, fists clenched tight. A surge of love so fierce it stole my breath, protective, primal, overwhelming. We named him after my wife's grandfather. First night home, I rocked him in the dark living room, house silent except for his soft breathing and the old rocker's creak. His small hand curled around my finger like a promise I hadn't earned. Fatherhood brought joy so bright it hurt, and terror just as sharp. I wanted to be present, steady, the man who showed up. The restlessness stayed low under the skin, waiting.

Sleeplessness crept back. Nights stretched longer, and the bottle moved closer. I sat with my baby boy asleep on my chest, a bottle of beer sweating on the side table, guilt coiling tighter with every sip. Partying, alcohol, and drugs filled gaps until the connection frayed—no explosive fights, just slow drift. My marriage ended in 1983. Divorce papers smelled of old coffee and ink, signed quietly. No screaming. Just the crushing weight of another failure. Joint custody at first, then full to me later when her life unraveled too. First night alone in a cramped apartment, the silence roared. No child's laughter. No wife's voice. Just the fridge's hum and the slow spin of the room. I sat on the couch with whiskey, tears coming down quietly and ugly, for a family broken, for the man I couldn't become.

My second marriage arrived fast, like a summer storm. I met her at the potato plant in Heyburn during a graveyard shift, eyes meeting across the breakroom table under flickering lights. She had a warm laugh, dark hair catching the dim glow. Every round through the plant, I'd stop, lean against her Hyster forklift, and make her laugh until the foreman barked. Dating began with dinners at the river-bridge lounge and drives along the Snake River with the windows down, cottonwood scent thick in the night air. We were married in a small ceremony at my parents' home. Dad officiated. The house smelled of polished wood and fresh flowers. I stood in the suit Dad had bought when I returned from Germany, heart pounding, promising forever. For a moment, everything felt right, hopeful, possible.

But cracks showed almost immediately. Elk hunt before the wedding, I loaded six cases of beer and a bottle of tequila into the camper. She noticed later, voice quiet. "I knew you drank, but I didn't realize how much."

I brushed it off, joking, deflecting. Arguments started small. Late nights at the armory. Money tight. Alcohol on my breath when I came home. Her disappointment cut deeper than any Article 15. "You're not here," she'd say, standing in the kitchen doorway while the boys slept.

I promised change, and for a while I did, cutting back, coming home early, playing with her two boys and my toddler building block towers, fixing bicycles when asked. Clean moments arrived, fragile and bright, like sunlight on the Payette after rain.

Our sons grew. Their grandpa and I taught them fishing on the Snake, little poles bobbing, excitement flashing in their eyes when trout tugged. Moments pure, like redemption glimpsed. But too often I arrived reeking or distracted, the bottle pulling even when I was physically present. Guilt became constant, a low-grade fever. My youngest would ask why Dad smelled funny, why Dad was always tired. His small hand in mine on river walks, tugging me toward the water like he could pull me back from the edge. I saw myself in him, the boy who once watched a bobber full of quiet wonder. Now I was the one drifting, bottle in hand, while he slept. Every blackout, every hangover chipped at that trust. I was failing him, failing to be the father who showed up sober, steady, and present.

I wanted better, for him, for us, for the man I still hoped I could become. But the pull proved stronger than my will. The bottle offered false comfort—warmth that never lasted, numbness that left me colder. Fights grew louder with doors slamming, voices rising, dinner burning on the stove. She cried in the kitchen, back turned. I'd leave, drive until anger faded, road humming under tires, headlights cutting the dark like accusations.

Simmering dread became a constant companion. I could feel the fractures widening, small at first, then deeper, threatening to split everything apart. Confusion choked me. How had I come so far from the riverbanks, from the turret where I'd felt invincible, only to end up here half-gone, chasing haze, watching trust dim in the eyes that mattered most? Love surged every time I looked at my family, yet fear whispered louder, *You're losing them. You're losing everything.* And the bottle waited, patiently, promising it could make the fear go quiet. But it never did.

Buddy Note

Coming home after the Army feels like stepping off a solid deck onto loose gravel with no orders, no crew, no clear mission except "figure it out." The quiet hits different with no engine rumble to drown racing thoughts, no battle buddy to call you on your bullshit.

For me, docks and college looked like forward motion, but the bottle found me faster than any job. One beer after shift became the new debrief, then the new normal.

First marriage, then our son, tiny fist around my finger, eyes full of trust, should've anchored me. Instead, drift pulled harder. I was there physically, but half-gone, chasing haze started in Kitzingen gasthauses. Guilt stacked quietly, every time his face dimmed when I walked in reeking, every promise broken to be the dad he deserved.

Second chance with her, of breakroom eyes, Snake River drives, and a small wedding, felt like a reset. Cracks hit fast. Late nights, heavy breath. "You're not here." Promised change. Cut back, played with the boys, clean moments, like old river light.

But the bottle waited. My guard anchored for two days, but the rest of the time belonged to the pull. Fights escalated with shouts and burned dinner. She cried and turned away. I drove. Sons grew. I taught fishing, trout tugging, eyes bright. They wanted a steady dad. Too often, I was gone, hungover. The guilt was heavy with trusting eyes dimming, a small hand tugging as if he could save me. I was breaking his wonder.

I wanted to stop, for them, myself. Didn't know how. Bottle lied, saying, Just unwind.

If you're that vet in the kitchen, partner hurting deep, kids' questions dodged, guilt thick, slide starts quiet. Extra pour. "Earned" late night. Morning "never again" pounding. Not unwinding, but a train speeding.

Don't wait till eyes dim forever or marriage flattens. Name it while they still care. Tell one straight shooter, a National Guard buddy, a chaplain, or a Vet Center (call 988 and press 1). One sentence of "Losing them, don't know how to stop," slows the train.

Chapter 11

Weekend Warrior

The Idaho National Guard armory in Burley became the only place left where the world still made sense. Every month, in the pre-dawn dark, I drove the long straight highway east from Heyburn, headlights cutting through frost that glittered like shattered glass across the sagebrush flats. The moment I pulled into the lot and killed the engine, the familiar assault hit, a low, throaty growl of M60 diesels idling in the bay, sharp metallic bite of gun grease hanging thick, hydraulic fluid's faint chemical sweetness mixing with diesel exhaust. Hatches clanged open, metallic echoes vibrating deep in my chest like a second heartbeat. For forty-eight hours, I shed the man I had become outside those walls. I wasn't the husband whose wife cried behind closed doors. I wasn't the father whose sons flinched at the smell on his breath when I walked in late. I was crew again. Loader. Gunner. Driver. Commander. Load. Aim. Fire. The ground shuddered under churning tracks. Dust boiled behind us in choking gray clouds. Voices crackled over intercoms, clipped, certain, alive. In that steel cocoon, the drift paused. I could almost believe I was still the man who once felt invincible inside fifty-two tons of rolling thunder.

The 116th Armored Cavalry, "Sneaky Snake," gave me temporary resurrection. We rolled out onto the endless sagebrush desert under Idaho's merciless sky, tracks grinding brittle brush into powder, exhaust rolling thick and acrid across the flats. Commander's voice cut through the headset like a blade. "Driver, advance! Gunner, target twelve o'clock!" Turret swung with hydraulic whine, crosshairs locking on distant silhouettes. Loader slammed the round home. A violent clang of brass meeting steel, breech locking with a final, heavy thud that rattled teeth.

"Up!" When the main gun spoke, recoil slammed us backward like a living thing. Cordite smoke burned eyes and throat, leaving a bitter metallic taste on the tongue. For those brief, roaring hours, reality returned—the same reverence I'd known as a boy when a catfish erupted in silver spray on the Payette, only now it was steel and diesel answering my hands. Love burned fiercely and wordlessly for these weekend brothers. We trusted each other with our lives every time the hatches sealed. I would not fail them. Not there. Not in the only place left where failure still carried a consequence that I could understand.

But on Sunday night, the spell always broke. The plant had closed for a good few months earlier. National Guard pay barely covered fuel and groceries. Stress coiled in my chest like rusted barbed wire, tighter with every unpaid bill, every sideways glance from my wife. Beer became ritual, after livestock auctions where ranchers' voices rose and fell like distant thunder, in the dusty cab after feeding, behind the barn at twilight when the light turned gold and accusing. Marijuana slipped back more often, then meth and opiates, heavier—hydrocodone first for the ache in my back from years of wrenching and hauling, then because the ache lived deeper, in the hollow where purpose used to be. Half-gallon vodka mornings arrived without warning. I'd stand at the kitchen counter staring at the bottle, amber liquid catching weak sunlight, and feel a cold, detached curiosity rise. *Why hasn't this killed me yet?* A darker part answered, *Maybe it still will.* Part of me welcomed the possibility.

My buddy Tiny, a big man, 400 pounds if he was an ounce, lived out north of town in the real countryside. He always had a few hogs around his place to raise and butcher, and every Saturday morning, he'd run weaner pigs through the livestock auction in town. Tiny bought them cheap, raised them for himself, and sold some to local 4-H program kids who'd show them at the county fair in the fall. I started heading out to his place early, before the sale, to help load whatever he was taking through the ring. We'd fill our to-go cups with whiskey and coffee, or whiskey and Coke, and hit the road. Day drinking started innocent enough with laughter in the cab, stories about plant days, bullshit about who could out-lift who. But the cups kept getting refilled. At the pens, in the truck, at the sale barn—it didn't matter where. We thoroughly enjoyed each other's company. The whiskey made everything feel looser, warmer, possible.

Eventually, those mornings turned into a regular ritual. Weekends messing around with pigs or dairy calves, sipping whiskey while we worked. Tiny's place smelled of manure, wet straw, and diesel from the old tractor. We'd lean on fence rails watching piglets scramble, passing the cup back and forth, talking about how the land out there felt different, open, quiet, far from town noise and judging eyes. One Saturday, half-drunk in the cab on the way back from the auction, the idea hit of why not buy more land than we'd planned? Skip the trailer court. Get a real farm. Raise calves bought at auction, sell them fat in the fall. A place to breathe. A place to belong again. Home had become a minefield wired to explode. My wife watched the changes with eyes that grew harder and colder each week of late nights when I stumbled in reeking of whiskey and smoke, mood swings that hit like sudden summer squalls, money vanishing into nothing. Arguments ignited without warning. Voices rose until the boys woke and stood frozen in the hallway, faces pale in the dim light leaking under their door. She cried in the kitchen, back turned, shoulders trembling with silent sobs that cut deeper than any shout. I'd grab keys, slam the screen door so hard the frame rattled, car engine roaring to life, headlights carving the black highway while anger bled out mile after mile. The road hummed beneath me, but the silence inside the cab screamed louder—accusation, shame, the slow realization that I was losing them one night at a time.

The National Guard weekends kept me tethered, but only for forty-eight hours. The rest of the time, the bottle waited, patient, velvet, promising it could quiet the roar inside, promising tomorrow I could still be the dad they needed, the husband she deserved. Tomorrow never came.

Buddy Note

Weekend warrior life of two days in the armory with diesel rumble, hatch clangs, crew trust felt like resurrection. For forty-eight hours, the drift stopped. I was crew again, not the guy whose family flinched when he walked in reeking. But Sunday night always came. National Guard pay thin, bills stacking, wife's eyes hardening, kids' small faces pale in hallway light. Bottle waited after auctions, behind barns, in cabs with buddies like Tiny, with whiskey and coffee turning day drinking into a ritual. "Just unwinding," I told myself. The same lie from Kitzingen gasthauses, and the same voice that whispered, One more won't hurt.

If you're that vet still chasing weekend structure of armory, range, and crew bonds to drown the weekday noise, the spell breaks Sunday night. Isolation creeps back. The bottle becomes your debrief. Kids' trust dims. Marriage frays. The train is building speed.

Don't wait till home is a minefield and tomorrow never comes. Name it while you still have crew around you. Tell one straight shooter, a National Guard battle buddy, a chaplain, a Vet Center (call 988, and press 1). One sentence of "Losing them, don't know how to stop," slows the train. Lean into the structure hard, but talk before the bottle becomes the only debrief. Discipline from motor pools and quals can protect what's under the armor if used early.

The river taught patience. Use it to listen, speak, fight for them and yourself. One sober Sunday, not too far gone. At the fork, choose the harder road that leads home.

CHAPTER 12

THE FARM

The farm had been a dream for a long time, a place to be with the land again, out in the country, my own little kingdom where the noise inside my head might finally quiet down. Tiny's place and our weekend rituals planted the seed deep. We'd load his stock early Saturday mornings, fill to-go cups with whiskey and coffee, and head out day drinking while messing with pigs or calves. Pens, truck cab, sale barn, didn't matter where, we thoroughly enjoyed each other's company. And the whiskey. During a half-drunk ride back from the auction, the idea crystallized. Forget the trailer court; we'd buy real acreage. Fatten up the calves there. A place that was really ours.

The wife and I had been eyeing a manufactured home, but what the hell—what's a few more acres? Because of those drinking sessions with Tiny, I ended up with eighty acres of lava-rock-scattered land east of town, in the middle of nowhere, Lava rock everywhere, black, jagged, stubborn—but the soil between held promise. FHA loan from plant savings and livestock deals secured it. A new manufactured home was placed on a gravel pad that we leveled ourselves. There we built our little farm and raised our family.

We put together about thirty breeding sows, forty acres of hay, and forty acres of pasture. The boys weren't sure at first with a new high school, girls, and friends, and now this far-out place where the nearest stoplight was twenty miles away. But the youngest took it. Chores gave him the structure of feeding, watering, and mucking pens. Work ethic grew in the rhythm of buckets clanging, gates creaking, animals breathing steam in cold mornings. It kept him out of trouble in town. We carefully and safely shot guns across the hay fields, teaching the boys handling, respect, and trigger discipline. They learned to hunt pheasants and doves in the cottonwoods along the draw, fond memories from when drinking hadn't yet caused deep family pain. Those afternoons carried me: boys' faces lighting up when a bird flushed, wings beating frantically, shotgun cracking sharp and final, soft weight of downed feathers in small hands. My love surged fiercely in those moments—I wanted them to carry this steadiness forward, to know land and work could anchor you when everything else shifted.

Spring was the best time. Kids from around the county would come out to pick their baby pigs for the fair in the fall. We'd open the pens with forty or fifty weaner pigs squealing, scrambling, pink and curious, and let the kids go in. They'd catch their own, laughing, getting muddy, arguing over which one was "theirs." Parents watched from the fence, smiling, thermos coffee in hand. The air smelled of fresh straw, warm piglets, and cut hay drying in the sun. For those hours, the farm felt alive, purposeful, right. I'd stand on the porch rail watching, cup of coffee in hand, sometimes spiked, sometimes not, chest swelling with something close to pride. This was working. This was mine. This was us.

But the bottle waited for me every evening. After chores, after irrigation pipes hissed and thumped, after hay bales stacked in the barn loft, I'd pour a pull, then another. Warmth spread, edges softened, the roar inside dulled. It wove tighter into routine, unnoticed at first. Morning coffee turned to whiskey-laced by noon on bad days. Evenings on the porch at dusk, shotguns cleaned and oiled beside me, rags heavy with solvent's sharp bite, bottle within easy reach on the rail. Sun sank behind river cottonwoods, long shadows stretching like fingers across empty fields. Birds fell quiet. Only wind moved through tall grass, distant cackles fading into dusk until silence swallowed everything. My hands still carried gun oil and blood. My heart sat heavy as wet clay in my chest.

Who was I kidding?

That land, those animals, those hunts were supposed to heal me, supposed to keep the bottle at arm's length, supposed to make me the father my boys could look up to without flinching, without catching the sour whiskey on my breath when I appeared on weekends. In every quiet moment, I saw the youngest's small hand tugging mine toward the river, eyes bright with that same pure wonder I once carried on the Payette docks, voice high with excitement when a trout struck. I was supposed to be the steady presence, the man who showed up sober and whole. Instead, I was the one drifting farther every day, chasing the bottle's false promise that one more pour would quiet the roar inside, that tomorrow I could still be the dad he needed.

I tried cold turkey once. Poured the vodka down the sink in gray dawn light, watched amber spiral away in furious eddies, empty jug staring back like a verdict. My hands shook so violently I dropped the first scoop of feed, and grains scattered across frozen ground like spilled promises. Sweat soaked my shirt in the cool air despite the chill. Birds cackled from the pens as if mocking. Three days. That was all. The ache returned—deeper, meaner, clawing at ribs and throat—until I broke and reached again.

Looking at my reflection in the porch window at dusk, my face older, hollower, eyes ringed with shadows I couldn't hide. The boy who once sat motionless on river docks asking why people fell had become a man falling slowly, deliberately. Every inch was chosen in the name of numbness. I whispered to the empty fields, to the darkening sky, to the sons I could still see in memory. *Tomorrow I'll stop. Tomorrow I'll be better. Tomorrow I'll be enough.* For them, for her, for the man I still desperately wanted to become. But tomorrow never came.

We never made much money. Hay prices dipped. Feed costs climbed. Vet bills stacked when sows got sick. Calves didn't always finish fat enough. The dream unraveled slowly, with missed payments, then notices, then bankruptcy papers smelling of ink and finality. The courtroom smelled of old coffee and furniture polish. The judge's voice was calm but firm. Assets liquidated. Land gone. Animals were sold off. My manufactured home moved. The illusion shattered.

But even as it failed, the farm gave us a good, safe place to raise the family during those years. It held us with chore rhythm for the boys, pheasant hunts in cottonwoods, spring pig sales full of kids' laughter, quiet evenings watching shadows stretch across fields. It gave me space to drink, yes, but also space to be with my sons before the drift pulled me too far. Love for them burned fiercely even through the haze as the fear of losing them whispered louder every night. Confusion choked every breath. How had the roar of tanks, the peace found in first holding my newborn son, the fierce love that once burned so bright, led me here, to a porch at twilight with a bottle in my hand and my children's faith slipping away like sand through open fingers?

I wanted to stop—for them, for myself—God, how I wanted it. But the bottle lied to me with velvet certainty. *Just unwind. Just this once. You've earned it.* And every time, I listened—until the listening became louder than love, louder than fear, louder than the last faint echo of the man I used to be.

Buddy Note

If you're that vet chasing a "reset" in land, a project, a move, or anything to outrun the drift, the bottle rides along. Escape laced with the thing you're running from. Kids' wonder dims when you reek. Marriage frays. Dream turns hollow. Train builds speed while you tell yourself, Tomorrow I'll stop.

Don't wait till land's gone, boys' faith slips, or tomorrow never comes. Name it, while the farm or whatever reset still holds you. Tell one straight shooter, an old National Guard buddy, a sponsor, or Vet Center (call 988, and press 1). One sentence of "Losing them, bottle's winning, don't know how to stop," slows the train. Lean into the good parts of chores, hunts, and family, but talk before the bottle becomes the only debrief.

The current teaches stillness. Use it—hear others, speak out, guard them and yourself. Keep your head while you still can. Where the trail splits, climb the steep one. It takes you back.

Chapter 13

Gold-Plated Trouble

What had started as a low-profile side venture, easy money on the weekends, quietly metastasized into a sprawling, high-stakes enterprise concealed behind the everyday appearance of the small-town meat-processing plant and its attached upland bird-hunting club.

From the county road the place still looked ordinary enough with rows of wire-mesh flight pens pulsing with the iridescent flash of pheasants and the rusty-brown dart of chukars strutting in morning light, their sharp cackles carrying across dry fields on the breeze, the low metallic hum of the walk-in freezer venting cold fog into sage-scented air, and the faint, mineral tang of blood and wet feathers drifting from the processing shed. Hunters pulled up in battered pickups on crisp fall mornings, shotguns slung easily over shoulders, thermos coffee steaming in callused hands, ready for a guided release and flush over the leased island in the middle of the Snake River. They left with coolers of dressed birds and stories for the bar in the small city of Heyburn. Legitimate enough, or close enough to pass in quiet farm country.

But legitimate work had dried up after the potato plant closed. The man who ran the outfit, a calculating mid-forties operator with a perpetually assessing stare and a teenage son who shadowed him like an apprentice, offered steady pay behind the scenes. At first, it felt like survival. I managed the bird pens, feeding and watering, moving shade tarps against the relentless sun, and building new flight enclosures with a staple gun and wire cutters until my palms were callused and blistered. Every other week, I drove the long highway to a much larger bird farm, loaded crates of fertile eggs and day-old chicks into the truck bed, then spent the return trip listening to the soft peeping and the rattle of cardboard against metal. Back at the farm, the day-olds went under precisely regulated brood lamps, temperature and humidity dialed so tight a few degrees either way meant losses. I placed the eggs carefully into the big old wooden incubator with dozens of special trays designed for gentle turning. Every day, I checked thermometers, candled for fertility, held my breath when the first pips appeared, and tiny beaks broke shell.

When hunters were booked, mostly wealthy out-of-state

clients, I rose in the dark, loaded cages onto the pontoon boat we'd bought secondhand, ferried birds across the Snake in pre-dawn blackness while the river ran black and muscular beneath the hull. The boat was big enough to carry the four-wheeler, dog crates, and supplies, too. I'd nose it onto the island gravel, unload in the gray light, release birds into cover, then wait at the dock as the hunting party arrived at first light, their coolers clinking. They were already laughing, reaching for cans of beer before the coffee even cooled. I handled the dogs as well, registered Labs, red Irish setters, German shorthairs, their physical care, daily exercise, transport to and from the island, the familiar comfort of wet fur and eager panting after a long morning in the field.

All of it—the boat runs in darkness, the sunburned hunters sipping from cans by noon, the dogs—was cover. Behind the unremarkable exteriors, separate outbuildings harbored the real operation of tightly controlled cultivation rooms glowing under banks of high-wattage lights on timers, ventilation fans scrubbing odor near-silently, and hydroponic reservoirs delivering exact nutrient doses with the soft click of solenoids. Starters under gentle halogens gave way to mature plants stretching four and five feet, heavy colas bowing under resin, the air inside thick with sweet-skunky perfume, the fans barely containing it. Night after night alone, I filled chicken-wire-and-garbage-bag pots with pallet-load potting mix hauled from out of town, planted three expensive "special" seeds per container, positioned them under the correct spectrum lamps, then watered endless rows so carefully I could almost feel each plant breathing.

The money flowed, reportedly to rich folks and celebrities up in Sun Valley, Ketchum, and Hailey, where movie stars had started buying taverns and sports bars. Bundles of $20 bills arrived in vacuum-sealed packs. At night, I counted them into careful stacks and buried the cash later out on the island under starlight and river murmur.

During those same summers, we carved out precious weeks to fly north to Kenai, Alaska, chasing salmon and halibut the way a drowning man reaches for air. The moment the plane's wheels left Boise's asphalt, the weight on my chest lifted a fraction. Below us, the brown sagebrush flats gave way to jagged white peaks, Cook Inlet glittering like hammered silver under late-June sun, glaciers hanging in the high country like frozen rivers caught mid-roar. When we touched down in Soldotna, the air hit different, sharp, clean, laced with spruce resin and salt. It smelled like possibility rather than buried cash and chicken-wire pots.

We stayed in a small cedar cabin on the Kenai River. Nothing fancy. Knotty-pine walls that creaked when the wind pushed off the water, a tiny kitchenette where coffee perked strong and black before dawn. Mornings started in the dark. Rain gear rustled like stiff paper as we layered fleece under bibs still damp from the day before. The river itself was alive, cold, muscular, the color of glacial silt, pushing past the dock with a low, steady growl that vibrated up through the planks into my boots. We'd motor out in a flat-bottom drift boat, the guide's voice low and steady. "Back-bounce the roe here . . . Watch the tip."

Then the hit. A chrome-bright king salmon would slam the bait like a freight train. The rod doubled over violently, line screaming off the reel in a high metallic whine that cut through the rush of water. My forearms burned instantly, my shoulders knotted, my heart beat fast against my ribs with that same raw adrenaline I once felt when the

M60 turret swung, and everything clicked. The fish swam downstream in powerful surges, head shaking so hard the rod tip blurred. When it finally tired and came boatside, its broad silver flank flashing, gill plates flaring red, the guide's gaff flashed and the deck erupted in shouts and laughter. The metallic tang of fresh blood mixed with river mud and diesel from the kicker motor. We bled them over the side, tails still twitching, then iced them in coolers that quickly turned pink.

Later in the summer, the silver salmon arrived, acrobatic, furious, leaping clear of the water in shiny arcs that caught the sun like thrown knives. Sockeye turned whole stretches of river blood-red. Their bites were so constant that the net never stayed dry. Halibut days were different beasts entirely, with full-day charters out of Homer. Two hours pounding into Cook Inlet, boat rocking in green swells, salt spray stinging cheeks and lips, Redoubt and Iliamna volcanoes looming like silent white gods on the horizon. Once on the grounds, the heavy sinkers dropped two, three hundred feet, and the wait began. Then the thump. Not a tap but a freight-train pull that nearly jerked the rod from your hands. Cranking against dead weight, legs braced on the slippery deck, back screaming, until that massive mottled-brown-and-cream body broke the surface, broad as a truck tire, marble eyes staring up, mouth gaping in silent protest. The deck exploded again with high-fives, whoops, and cameras clicking, while the mate gaffed and bled the fish, blood running in thick ropes across the white fiberglass.

By evening, we'd be back at the dock, arms rubbery, fingers cramped, the sweet-smoky smell of alder chips already drifting from the smokehouse where fillets hung in long rows. One night, I grilled fresh king steaks over an open fire, skin crisp, flesh flaky and rich, butter melting into the pink meat. And for a few hours, the world narrowed to the crackle of flames, the river murmuring behind us, and the clean, honest exhaustion in my muscles. My wife and kid never came on these trips because money and school schedules were tight, and I told myself it was better that way. But sitting there with grease on my hands and the taste of wild salmon on my tongue, memories would surge so hard it hurt. I wanted them there, laughing beside me, with my boy's small hands gripping a rod, his eyes wide when a fish hit. Instead, I was chasing this wholesome joy alone, knowing the extra cash that paid for the plane tickets came from vacuum-sealed bundles of cash buried on the island and plants glowing under artificial sun back home.

The contrast cut like a fillet knife. For those precious weeks the bottle stayed mostly corked—just one cold beer at day's end, nothing more—and the hidden grow rooms, the buried money, the lies I told my family all felt distant. Quiet awe returned, the same reverence I'd known as a boy watching a red-and-white bobber dance on the Payette, or inside the M60 when the crew clicked, and the gun roared true. In those moments, I could almost believe I was still the man capable of pure joy, of showing up whole.

But the flight home always brought that weight back on my chest. Mountains receded, Idaho's familiar brown flats rose from the horizon, and the old dread settled inside me like wet concrete. The cabin door would close behind me, and the glow of those hidden rooms would be waiting, timers clicking, the bottle of alcohol on the counter promising it could ease the transition. I told myself the trips proved I could still feel something real. And they did. But they also reminded me, with merciless clarity, how far I had drifted from that version of myself—and how much I was willing to risk to keep pretending I hadn't.

Those Kenai summers were mercy in disguise, brief windows of salt air and silver flashes that kept a small, stubborn spark alive when everything else tried to snuff it out. Without them, I'm not sure the climb back would have even been possible.

From the road, it looked innocent, with pheasants flashing in the sun, hunters laughing over coffee, dogs happy after a flush. Easy money, right? Managing birds, running the pontoon before dawn, turning eggs, watering rows at night. It felt like control. But a bottle waited after long days, a cold pull to quiet the ache, whispering, *You've got this.*

Alaska trips were a mercy nobody deserved. Sharp spruce air, river growling under the dock, salt spray on lips. Rod doubling when a king hit, forearms burning, heart hammering, untainted, halibut decks slick with blood. Alder smoke at dusk, salmon steaks hissing over the fire, crisp skin, butter melting into pink flesh. For weeks, the hidden rooms felt distant, buried cash forgotten. I wanted my boy there, his small hands on a rod, eyes wide at the strike. Instead, I chased that joy alone, plane tickets paid with vacuum-sealed bundles of cash and plants glowing under lamplight back home.

Buddy Note

If you're running a double life—surface legit, something darker humming underneath, telling yourself, Just until things steady, bottle or pipe ready to take the edge—listen. Plates don't spin forever. Mercy windows of river, salt air, and clean exhaustion are real but brief. Hold the spark they leave. That flicker kept me breathing when the haze tried to kill it.

Don't wait for the raid, cuffs, or dust-pluming cruisers in the mirror. Name it now while the illusion still feels solid. Tell one straight shooter who won't bullshit you, like a battle buddy, a sober vet, a sponsor, a Vet Center. Say out loud, "Deeper in than I admit. Scared I'm losing what matters." One sentence slows the train.

In the system of booking, court, or cell, say six words: "I'm a veteran—please flag VJO." It brings real help, not another cycle. Is your head loud? Call 988 now and press 1 for the Veterans Crisis Line, 24/7. Boise Rescue Mission (208) 343-2389 in Idaho. Hold on for one more night. Tell someone you served. Discipline from basic training and motor pool can carry you through to one honest reach. The river still flows. Grace finds cracks. The rise is closer than the dread would have you believe.

CHAPTER 14

THE RAID

The first crack appeared far from the property. A wildlife enforcement officer purchased restricted smoked salmon and game meat from a roadside vendor at a gun show several states away. Laboratory analysis confirmed the origins of illegally harvested wild Alaskan salmon and big-game animals. Investigators traced subsequent sales at other gun shows and exhibitions back to the northeast Burley facility. Search warrants were secured—not for the plants at first, but for records of who had supplied the prohibited meat and fish. They had been watching quietly for months, building the case piece by piece, waiting for the right trigger.

Dawn broke cold and clear on the morning when everything unraveled. I had just finished the overnight watering cycle, hoses hissing softly among the clicking timers, nutrient solution gurgling through lines, when I stepped outside and climbed into my truck. The sky was still bruised purple in the east, air sharp with frost and the faint diesel tang from the processing shed. I turned the key, engine coughing to life, and pulled off the gravel lane onto the county road blacktop. In the rearview mirror, movement caught my eye, a line of dark SUVs and marked cruisers accelerating hard out of the pre-dawn gloom, dust pluming behind them like smoke from a grass fire. My heart thumped hard against my ribs, and the wheel grew slick under sweating palms. I kept my eyes forward, refusing to turn, refusing to acknowledge the freight train closing the gap. Every mile felt like borrowed time, the engine's hum suddenly too loud, my pulse roaring in my ears.

They hit the property with overwhelming force. Idaho Fish and Game, Idaho State Police, and Drug Enforcement Administration agents swarmed in coordinated waves, boots crunching gravel, doors slamming, voices sharp over radios. Inside one of the main freezers, ostensibly packed with legitimate cuts of meat, they discovered kilo bricks of frozen marijuana buds, firearms, and thick stacks of currency rubber-banded together. That single find triggered immediate secondary warrants. Behind the pheasant-rearing pens, officers located concealed doors leading to the main cultivation areas, expansive windowless chambers filled floor-to-ceiling with three-foot plants under blazing artificial sunlight. In another building, another hidden entrance revealed hundreds of eight- to twelve-inch juveniles thriving under the same sophisticated setup. A third structure fronted what appeared to be a legitimate egg incubator for the hunting club's birds, but behind a false wall stood 1,236 mature plants, four to five feet tall, poised for final harvest.

The inventory process stretched across days. Adjacent counties executed related warrants at off-site locations, seizing additional evidence. Officials from state, city, and county governments toured the dismantled rooms, some visibly shaken by the scale of operations. One commissioner called it "a sad descent into degradation." Another admitted the size was an eye-opener. The local mayor framed the bust as proof that coordinated vigilance could dismantle even deeply embedded criminal enterprises, vowing that stiff penalties would send an unmistakable message.

All arrestees were held without bond pending arraignment. The primary operator received a multi-year indeterminate prison sentence, followed by additional time for possession with intent to deliver, plus separate penalties for the wildlife violations, including a lengthy revocation of hunting privileges after four deer were discovered on-site. Massive fines were imposed on top of the cash already confiscated. His son received a comparable term. Heavy equipment arrived within months to strip out the grow lights, ventilation systems, and hydroponic arrays. The once-bustling facility stood empty, a hollow shell stripped for parts.

I walked away without formal charges—insufficient direct evidence tying me to the operation, and I wasn't present during the initial sweep—but the escape felt hollow, like dodging a bullet only to realize the gun was still loaded and pointed at my head. The operation vanished overnight. So did the last fragile pretense of control I had clung to.

The dependency that remained in my shadow since

Germany now stood naked in daylight—liquor to quiet racing thoughts, pills to blunt the stress that never relented. I withdrew further, isolating myself even from the people who still cared. The abyss no longer loomed on the horizon; it had opened beneath my feet. The farm, the birds, the illusion of a reset life, all gone in the dust of those accelerating cruisers. I had chosen the dim glow over the light, the secret over the truth, and now the bill had come due.

Buddy Note

Heyburn looked normal from the road, with pheasants strutting, freezers humming, hunters laughing over coffee. Behind it, thousands of plants under hot lights, timers clicking, resin thick enough to taste. Bottle dulled the ache, whispered, Still in control. Wildlife bust on illegal game traced back like a slow fuse. A dawn raid of SUVs in the mirror, dust pluming, heart hammering. The swarm found frozen bricks, guns, cash, and hidden "grow rooms" glowing like bad dreams. I watched it for months. Property seized and stripped bare. The operator and his son were given harsh sentences. I walked—no tight tie—but illusion dead. The long chain of beer after stables, a drag behind the barn, a recoil in the turret, "A few plants won't hurt," echoing Germany's package lie, until lights were ripped out and silence hit harder than any sergeant's shout. If the grow room is humming or SUVs are closing in your rearview, stop saying you've got the wheel. The lie waits for higher stakes and louder shame. The train hits one ordinary dawn. Name it now. Tell a straight shooter, a battle buddy, a sober vet, a Vet Center (call 988 and press 1). One line saying, "Deeper in than admitted, scared," derails it. At booking, say, "Veteran—flag Veteran Judicial Outreach." It opens the treatment door. I lost a farm, years, almost everything—no chance to climb then. The river carves through the silt, and so can you, with one call. Hold on. Tell someone.

Chapter 15

Trucking

After the farm illusion shattered in 1999, trucking felt like a second chance at the dream I'd carried since high school of the open road, miles unspooling under tires, no one telling me where to be or when. I'd pumped gas near West Yellowstone as a kid, watching semis roll past like kings of the highway, drivers waving from high cabs with that quiet confidence I envied. Then, in my forties, I finally had my Class A commercial driver's license and a seat behind the wheel. Long hauls through the Northwest from Idaho to Washington, Oregon, Montana, sometimes down into Utah, with potatoes, lumber, frozen goods. The cab smelled like diesel, old coffee, and the faint pine air that slipped through the vents when I cracked the window on high passes. Radio low, CB crackling with trucker talk, engine humming steady under me. For the first few months, it felt like freedom again. Solitude that I could control. No crew to disappoint, no family to fail—just me, the road, and the next mile marker.

But solitude has teeth.

Days started before dawn with pre-trip inspection in truck-stop lots under sodium lights, flashlight beam sweeping tires, checking air lines, oil dipstick slick black on my fingers. I climbed in, fired the engine, a deep rumble vibrating through the seat, mirrors fogging with breath. I pulled out onto the interstate as the sky turned pink over the Sawtooth or Bitterroot mountain ranges. Coffee from a Thermos, black and bitter, steam rising against the windshield. Miles rolled easily at first with sagebrush flats giving way to mountain curves, rivers glinting far below. I'd crank the window down on descents, let cold air rush in, which tasted like freedom. Radio stations faded in and out, and sometimes I'd sing along to old country, voice rough, alone.

Nights flipped it. Truck-stop neon buzzing, grease-thick air in the diner, cigarette smoke curling under sodium lamps, semis idling like sleeping beasts. I'd park in the back row, engine off, cab suddenly too quiet. The bottle waited in the sleeper berth. One beer to unwind after twelve hours of white-line fever. Then two. Whiskey chased the ache in my back caused by bad seats and bad roads.

Insomnia came back worse than ever. The same nights I used to sleep through artillery sims in Germany now stretched endlessly. A doctor prescribed 10 mg of Ambien to knock me out clean. At first, it worked. Pill down with water or beer if the day had been rough. Light out in the sleeper, engine idling low like white noise. I woke up eight hours later, head clear, ready for the next load.

Then tolerance crept in. One pill stopped cutting it. Two became routine. And when I chased them with whiskey—to force the sleep faster, to quiet the GERD[1] burn and the guilt that roared louder at night—the blackouts started.

The first one I noticed was small. I woke up in the bunk, the cab dark except for the dashboard glow. An empty beer can was on the floor. Half a bag of chips was scattered across the console like confetti. Crumbs on my shirt. No memory of eating. Just a fuzzy gap where hours should have been. I laughed it off, thinking, *Must've been hungry in my sleep*. I told myself it was nothing. But the blackouts got bigger.

One night outside Boise, after a brutal run through snow over Lolo Pass, I popped two Ambien with a pull from the flask. Blackout. Next thing I knew, I woke up behind the wheel. Truck parked crooked in a rest-area pullout, engine running, headlights cutting through the fog, radio playing static. My hands were on the wheel like I'd been driving. My heart thumped so hard, and I tasted metal. I checked the mirrors. No dents, no cops. But the odometer had jumped twenty miles. Twenty miles that I didn't remember. I sat there shaking, staring at the dark highway, wondering what I'd done, who I'd almost hit, and if I'd crossed the center line.

Another time in Utah, at a truck stop near Salt Lake, I came to on the bunk with the door unlocked, boots off, a half-eaten burger wrapper on my lap from the diner I didn't remember walking to, and grease on my fingers.

1 Gastroesophageal reflux disease.

I no memory of ordering, paying, or eating. No receipt. Just the taste of onions lingering and a cold sweat that the cab heater couldn't burn off. I locked the door, wiped my hands on my jeans, and stared at the ceiling until dawn. The road that used to feel like freedom now felt like a trap—every blackout miles I couldn't account for, every pill a step closer to losing my commercial driver's license (CDL), the last thing keeping me moving.

The worst were the conversations I didn't have. CB crackling at 0300, some driver asking if I was okay, saying I'd been keying up, talking nonsense about river bottoms and sons who didn't call anymore. I didn't remember pressing the mic. I didn't remember the words. Just woke to the static and the shame of knowing I'd been "there" but not really.

Mixing Ambien with alcohol turned the blackouts into something darker. The drug's label warned against it—central-nervous-system depressants stacking, breathing slowing, judgment gone—but warnings don't hit until you wake up wondering if you're still alive. I'd wash the pill down with whiskey to force sleep faster, and wake with no memory. But evidence was everywhere, with my truck in park at a weigh station I didn't recall stopping at, my phone log showing a call to an ex-wife at 0200 and my voicemail full of slurred apologies I didn't remember making), or once, finding the cab door open to cold mountain air, me standing outside in socks, staring at stars like I'd been sleepwalking the parking lot.

Each blackout chipped away at the dream. The road wasn't open anymore—it was a black void where I disappeared. The cab that once promised control now felt like a rolling blackout chamber. I kept driving because stopping meant facing the fact that my childhood fantasy of long-haul freedom had become a slow-motion wreck. Miles rolled, but I was losing ground every night.

The DUIs piled up slowly, then fast. First in Minidoka County, pulled over outside of Rupert, personal rig, not the company truck. A flashlight in my face, the officer's voice calm. "Step out, sir." The breath test beeped angrily—way over. Cuffs cold, ride to the station silent except for radio chatter. Fines, court costs, and suspension of my regular license. CDL stayed for a while. I told myself it was a wake-up call. Paid the fees. Kept driving.

But the pull was stronger than the promise. Second DUI in Canyon County, coming home from a run, bottle in the passenger seat. Red-and-blue lights in the mirror again. Same script of field sobriety on the road's shoulder, wind whipping sagebrush, my balance and the breathalyzer failing. More fines. Longer suspension. Still no treatment push—just pay and move on. Shame settled heavier, and the bottle waited at the next stop.

My National Guard years ended around then, ten years honorable with the 116th, no more weekend diesel roars or crew bonds. Structure was gone. The cab became my last anchor. I leaned harder into it with longer hauls and more nights out.

The final one broke everything.

I finished a long run, a northwest loop, bone tired. Home alone, I needed sleep so badly. Took Ambien, chased it with beer. Blackout. Woke to two police officers speaking to me while I was knocking on a barbershop door at the local mall. I was standing there in my clothes from the day before, my truck parked crooked in the lot. No memory. They asked questions I couldn't answer. Cuffs again. I failed my breath test. License revoked—CDL gone—permanent for a commercial driver after that stack of DUIs.

Idaho law didn't play around. One DUI on a CDL meant a one-year disqualification minimum, while multiples meant a lifetime ban if patterns held. My childhood dream of long-haul freedom, an open road, and being king of the highway was stripped away in a mall parking lot I didn't remember driving to.

Court dates blurred after that. Orange jumpsuit again, chains rattling. The judge's voice said, "This ends here." No more runs. No more miles. Just me, the bottle, the pipe when meth crept back, pills to blunt the edge. Mind rabbit-trailed on the past—Germany gasthauses, farm lights, sons' dim eyes—while wondering why it wasn't killing me and not caring if it did.

The cab had been my last illusion, miles rolling while circling the drain, from Germany blackouts to Kitzingen pours to farm grow rooms to truck-stop neon. The road that once promised escape now just took me farther from everything that mattered.

Buddy Note

If blackouts are hitting—waking to evidence you were "there" but not really—stop saying "just tonight." Pull over. Flush the rest. Reach out to the VA or a sober vet. Call 988 and press 1. One call before the next blackout. The road can wait. Your life can't.

The cab became the last illusion of miles rolling while circling the drain, from blackouts in Germany to Kitzingen pours to farm lights to truck-stop neon.

GERD burning, depression thick. Mind looped—turrets, sons' dim eyes, wondering why it wasn't fatal. I stopped caring.

If you're parked at a truck stop right now, bottle in the sleeper, telling yourself, Just tonight, or staring at another suspension knowing the CDL's next—the slide is quiet until it isn't. Isolation fuels it. No crew, no eyes on you except the mirror you dodge.

Don't wait for the next DUI, ER, or blackout you can't explain. Pull over safely and reach out. Call 988 and press 1 for the Veterans Crisis Line, 24/7, no judgment. Find a truck-stop Alcoholics Anonymous (AA) or Narcotics Anonymous (NA) if posted, or call a sober vet or Legion brother.

Tell one straight person, a sponsor, an old battle buddy, or a VA outreach.

Discipline from qualifiers, stables, and long days can carry you through one call. I lost the wheel, almost everything. The Walmart parking lot wasn't a grave—it was the floor I pushed from. It can be yours, too, with one reach. The rise is closer than it feels. Hold on. Tell someone you served. We're still out here—no one left behind.

PART III

Recovery

Chapter 16

The Road Back

So there I was again, sitting in a cell that had started to feel like the only home I deserved. Twin Falls County Jail, March through September 2015; 197 days that stretched like wet rope—slow, heavy, impossible to hurry. The first week, I counted every clang of the doors. By week three, I stopped. Time didn't move forward there; it just sat on your chest until you learned to breathe under it.

The routine never varied. Lights on at 0500, harsh

fluorescents that never dimmed, buzzing like distant artillery. Breakfast trays slid through the slot with cold oatmeal congealed into gray paste, a bruised apple, weak coffee that tasted like rust. I ate because the body demanded it, not because I wanted to. Mid-morning count, I stood at the bars, hands visible, eyes forward, while deputies walked the tier calling numbers. Afternoon court runs for those with hearings, with orange jumpsuits, belly chains rattling like loose change, ankles shackled so you could only shuffle. I went a few times early on. Stale coffee and lemon polish hung in the air. Judge Harris sat high on the bench, voice calm but firm. When my turn came, he looked down at the file, then at me.

"You're refusing bail again, Mr. Lineberry?"

"Yes, Your Honor."

"Why?"

I swallowed. The chain tugged at my wrists. "Nowhere to go, sir. Lost everything. Figured I'd wait till something real showed up—a program, not just another street."

He studied for me for a long time. "You're a stubborn man. But smart enough to know when you're out of moves."

A small nod.

"Remanded. Next appearance in thirty."

Back to the block. The hallway light never changed, a thin yellow strip cutting across the concrete floor from the corridor bulb. At night, it was the only thing that moved with shadows from passing deputies stretching and shrinking across the cell. I'd lie on the thin mat, back against the cold cinderblock, watching that line like it held answers. Sometimes it felt like the river bottoms back in Emmett—patient, carving slow—but without the peace. Just waiting. Waiting for court, for a letter, for anything that wasn't more of the same.

The bunks around me kept emptying and filling with strangers. Once the lights died, I'd catch why they'd been booked—a wreck, a barroom swing, money that never cleared. Down the row a man's breath broke into sobs. Mine held. I sat in my own silence, tracing how I'd ended up here. Weeks blurred into months on those thin mats. Family never visited. Not once. And then the worst news came. Dad passed away due to complications during heart surgery. The one who had always stood by me, the one I had disappointed so shamelessly. The news came through a guard—flat, final. Pain hit like a tank round. No visit, no goodbye. The court granted temporary release, directly to my son at the jail. He brought me a suit, and I changed into it before we left. The ankle monitoring bracelet stayed locked on under my pant leg. My son—grown, strong—stood right beside me the whole time. He kept his hand on my shoulder, steady and sure.

During the service, a young relative stood and pointed at me, voice shaking with anger. He blamed my drinking and my trouble for the stress that helped kill Dad. The words cut deep. Some heads nodded. Shame burned through me. I stood there in the suit my son had brought me, bracelet hidden but felt with every breath and movement. My son squeezed my shoulder and whispered, "Ignore it." Those two words held me up. The service ended, and I hugged him once, hard. Then he drove me back to the jail. The cell door closed again. Alone with the walls, the echo of those accusing words, and the steady pressure of my son's hand on my shoulder—the one thing that told me I wasn't completely lost.

Late June, everything shifted.

A social worker from the Veterans Justice Outreach (VJO) program visited me. The guards walked me to the visiting room, a small booth with scratched Plexiglas and metal stools bolted to the floor. She sat on the other side, in her mid-forties, with calm eyes, a VA badge clipped to her blazer. No judgment in her face. Just presence.

"Mr. Lineberry? I'm with VJO. Probation and parole flagged you as a veteran. We're here to help if you want it."

I stared at her through the glass. Voice rusty from disuse. "What kind of help?"

She slid a packet through the slot. "Boise Rescue Mission. New Life Program. Year-long, faith-based, in-house. Structure, counseling, work ethics, spiritual guidance, and job prep. It's not easy, but it's real. Not another thirty-day spin cycle."

I opened the folder with shaking hands. Pages smelled of fresh ink. Daily routine. Bible study. Group sessions. Kitchen duty. Financial classes. Graduation stats showed hundreds of men who'd walked out sober, employed, connected. I read every word twice. The hallway light flickered in my memory—not as an accusation anymore, but as a door that might open.

"You're eligible," she said. "VA can transport you if accepted. But you must apply. And mean it."

I looked up. "I mean it."

She nodded once. "Then fill this out. I'll be back tomorrow."

That night, I sat under the fluorescent buzz of the common area, pen scratching across the application. Name, service history, addiction timeline, and why I wanted to go in. I wrote the truth with no polish, no excuses. Germany cracks. Farm bust. My sons, whom I'd failed. The Walmart parking lot. The weight in my chest eased a fraction with every line—not gone—just lighter.

She came back the next day. Took the packet. "We'll

push it through fast."

On July 9, the acceptance letter arrived in a thin envelope. My hands shook as I opened it. "Approved. Start date immediately upon release."

July 16, Judge Harris called me up one last time. Chains off for the hearing—first time in months, my wrists felt naked.

"Application approved," he said. "Boise Rescue Mission. You still want this path?"

"Yes, Your Honor."

He looked at me then—really looked. "Then go take it. Don't come back here, Mr. Lineberry."

I was released that afternoon. A VA van waited outside the sally port. I stepped into the sunlight that hurt my eyes after months of artificial glare. The driver, a quiet vet in his fifties, nodded once. "Buckle up. Long ride to Boise."

I climbed in. The door shut. The engine started. We pulled onto the highway. Windows down. Fresh air rushed in past sagebrush, pine, and hot asphalt. No bleach. No metal bars. Just wind and sky and the slow realization that I wasn't dead yet.

The van hummed north. Mountains blurred past. I leaned my head against the glass, watching the river valleys open up to Payette, Boise, familiar shapes from childhood. The numbness that had owned me for decades began to subside—not gone, but slowly releasing.

Rock bottom met grace. The DUI wasn't the end; it was the break that forced the turn. Without VJO reaching into that cell, the spiral might have ended me in a parking lot or a ditch. Instead, it ended with clean air through an open window and a folder on my lap that promised structure, dignity, and a road back.

I had spent years running from the cracks in Germany,

from the shame of the hash and heroin I'd barely escaped from failing my boys and my family. The bottle had been both an escape and a prison. In that jail cell, with nothing left—no farm, no marriage, no illusions—I finally had to face the man in the mirror. I hated what I saw.

But beneath the hate, anger stirred—not at the world, but at my choices. I was angry that I'd let drift win for so long. Angry that I'd let the bottle define me.

And in that anger, a spark. Faint. Stubborn. I didn't want to die in that car. I didn't want to be the man who never came back. I wanted to live. To be present. To be the father my boys deserved—even if late. That spark was enough.

Buddy Note

Twin Falls jail with 197 days on thin mats, bleach smell, mystery-meat trays, graffiti walls, hallway light slicing the floor every night. Patterns were the same, with illusion shattered and losses mounting. I chose the bottle over everything. Shame sat heavy, with nowhere to hide. I refused bail, a stubborn terror mixed with faint hope that a real path would appear. Judge Harris said, "Stubborn but smart."

Late June, a VJO social worker walked into the visiting room. The New Life Program packet landed like a lifeline. A year-long faith-based recovery program, with structure, counseling, work, and dignity. One conversation, one application under buzzing lights, one acceptance letter, July 9.

Released July 16. VA transport to Boise, clean air rushing through the window after months of stink, the smell of sagebrush and pine replacing bleach.

River of Life shelter had coffee, clean linens, and a neon "Jesus Saves" on the corner. My VA exam found a six-month-old silent heart attack, another scar from the abuse. Rock bottom met grace. The DUI wasn't the end; it was an intervention I'd run from since Germany.

If you're on that mat tonight, chains rattling in your head, shame screaming, you're not too far gone or the sum of your worst nights. Shame's loud because it's held the mic too long.

Say six words at booking or court: "I'm a veteran—please flag VJO." You can find someone who throws a real rope rather than another cycle. Call 988 now and press 1 for a Vet Center, call a sober Legion vet, or call Boise Rescue Mission at (208) 343-2389 if in Idaho. Hold on for one more night. Tell someone you served. Discipline from basic training, motor stables, and border alerts can carry you through these hours toward one honest reach. The rise is not as far away as you think.

Chapter 17

A New Life Program at the Mission

The doors of the Boise Rescue Mission's River of Life shelter swung open on that blistering July afternoon in 2015. I stepped across the threshold carrying a small duffel of donated clothes, the sour residue of jail bleach still clinging to my skin, with a hope so fragile it felt like it might shatter if anyone looked at it too long. The lobby smelled of fresh coffee brewing in a giant urn, clean linens stacked on a folding table, and something faintly sweet, maybe the lemon cleaner they used on the tile. After 197 days of concrete, fluorescent buzz, and the constant metallic tang of despair, the fruity scent hit like grace itself, ordinary, warm, alive. My heart beat rapidly against my ribs with equal parts terror and relief. Freedom should have felt like release. Instead, it felt like standing on the edge of a cliff with no idea whether the next step was solid ground or empty air.

A Veterans Justice Outreach social worker had thrown the rope. Her visit to the jail's scratched Plexiglas visiting booth weeks earlier still burned in my memory, her calm eyes behind wire-rimmed glasses, a VA badge clipped to her blazer, no judgment in her voice when she slid the New Life Program packet through the slot. "Year-long. Faith-based. In-house. Structure, counseling, work, dignity. It's real, Don. Not another thirty-day spin." I'd read every page twice under the hallway's thin yellow light, hands shaking so badly the paper rattled. Daily routine. Bible study. Group sessions. Kitchen duty. Financial classes. Graduation numbers showed hundreds of men who'd walked out sober, employed, reconnected. The hallway light had flickered then—not as an accusation anymore, but as the faintest crack where something brighter might slip through.

Now I stood inside that promise. A staff member, with broad shoulders and a gentle voice, led me down a short hallway. "Welcome home, brother." The words landed softly but heavily. Home. I hadn't known what that word meant in years.

The New Life Discipleship and Recovery Program gripped me from the first morning. Wake up at 0600 sharp, feet hitting cold tile, body still aching from withdrawal's lingering claws. Morning devotions in the dining hall, with steam rising from coffee mugs and low voices reciting together, "I can do all things through Christ who strengthens me." The words landed on parched soil inside me. Tears came without warning—hot, silent, sliding down cheeks I hadn't let anyone see wet since childhood. For years, I'd drowned emptiness in vodka, meth, pills. There, in a circle of weary men who smelled faintly of soap and shared cigarettes they weren't allowed to smoke anymore, I felt exposed yet strangely held. Chapel services later swelled with hymns, "Amazing Grace," "It Is Well," that echoed off cinderblock walls, and for the first time in decades, a flicker of peace brushed against the raw places inside. The moment stole my breath. Maybe redemption wasn't a fairy tale. Maybe it was just showing up one more morning when every instinct screamed to run.

The mental work cut deepest and hurt most. Group sessions took place in a windowless classroom that smelled of sweat, coffee, and vulnerability. Folding chairs arranged in a rough circle. Fluorescent tubes buzzed overhead. I shared in halting fragments at first—Germany's first cracks, the heroin I'd chased twice and barely escaped, the unreported assault in basic that still woke me gasping some nights, DUIs stacking like unpaid debts, the 1999 farm raid that stripped the last illusion of control, sons whose eyes dimmed when I walked in reeking. Each admission felt like tearing off scabbed skin. Listening to other men, veterans, ex-cons, fathers who'd lost everything, the realization that I wasn't alone in the isolation settled heavily. Tears flowed freely, mine mingling with theirs as we mapped addiction's roots—unmet needs, buried trauma that turned to self-medication, the lie that numbness could ever fill what words and love never reached.

Relapse-prevention classes charted the triggers I'd ignored for decades—stress, loneliness, the bottle's velvet promise. We learned to interrupt the cycle with accountability, safe relationships, honest naming of fantasy, anxiety, self-pity, tension, excitement, and rationalization on the FASTER scale. The recovery workbook became my nightly companion, pen scratching across pages under a dim desk lamp, naming subconscious fears of "not enough," or "you'll always fall," faulty beliefs rooted in survival from Army days of "numb it or break." The agony of facing the father I'd become—choosing haze over my sons' trusting eyes—nearly undid me. One session, I broke completely, voice cracking as I admitted every broken promise, every missed birthday, every time I'd chosen the bottle over bedtime stories. Sobs shook me so hard the chair creaked. A brother across the circle reached out, hand heavy on my shoulder. "Been there, man. You're not alone." In that callused, steady touch, hope ignited. Not fleeting, but real, burning away layers of despair I'd carried so long I'd forgotten what joy felt like.

Physically, the program rebuilt me through labor that echoed the discipline of basic training but carried a gentler purpose. Kitchen duty, washing hundreds of trays, scrubbing pots until my hands pruned and ached, soapy water splashing against forearms. Maintenance tasks, stripping wax from floors, painting cinderblock walls eggshell white, taught dignity in honest sweat. Financial classes forced me to stare at budgets, every penny accounted for, rather than letting dollars vanish into liquor bottles. Job-search prep, resumes rewritten without shame, and mock interviews that left palms slick, built confidence I hadn't felt since qualifying on the range. Mission service pulled me outward: turkey drives in crisp fall air, hauling frozen birds into vans while breath fogged the windows; the speedway with race car engines thundering like old tanks, fundraising money; holiday banquets, setting up long tables, folding chairs heavy in my arms, the smell of turkey and gravy filling the hall. Each act of giving chipped away self-absorption, replaced it with gratitude so sharp it hurt.

Daily classes demanded vulnerability that turned strangers into brothers bound by shared scars. We met in quiet rooms thick with pain and encouragement, laughter breaking through sobs, hands reaching when someone couldn't speak. I graduated in May 2016 in a packed community hall, with firm handshakes, crisp certificates, and fresh flowers on stage, blooming bright against cinderblock. Pride and aching joy swelled until my chest hurt. I interned as an administrative assistant during the final months. Soon after, I was hired full-time as a front desk receptionist, living upstairs as in-house staff until 2021. Greeting guests, men whose eyes mirrored my old despair, became daily repayment, with a nod, a listening ear, "a hand up, not a handout," as Reverend Bill Roscoe always said. Every "Welcome, brother" I spoke carried the echo of the day someone had said it to me.

The New Life Program was grace dressed up in work boots—structure when I had none, dignity when I'd lost mine, community when isolation had nearly finished me. Scars remained in nightmares that still woke me gasping, stomach burning when stress rose, memory gaps from years of abuse, and the introversion that made crowds feel like enemy territory. But the emptiness that once howled inside had been filled—not perfectly, not instantly, but steadily—with purpose, faith, and men who refused to let me disappear again.

If you're reading this from a cell, a car, or a porch with

a bottle in reach, the door is open. The application is simple—call (208) 343-2389 or download it from boiserm.org—but the commitment changes everything. It's raw. It's hard. It's real. I'm a man who hit bottom in a Walmart parking lot, but walked through it and came out the other side. So can you.

Buddy Note

July 2015, I entered River of Life post-jail. Coffee, clean linens—grace hit—Veterans Judicial Outreach assistance.

Outreach delivered an application, acceptance, and a VA ride with fresh air.

A new life, a year-long faith-based rebuild, strict, spiritual, mental, and physical. Wake-up calls at 0600, devotions, hymns. Tears fell on dry ground.

Real groups where I shared Germany cracks, buried assault, DUIs, farm loss, sons' dim eyes. Vets nodded, knowing the same isolation. Brother's hand after family-fail breakdown: "Been there."

Work restored dignity through pots scrubbed, faucets fixed, pennies budgeted.

Service outward consisted of drives, fundraisers, and banquets. Giving replaced shame with gratitude.

Graduated in 2016 with a certificate, full of pride and grief. I continued as a staff member, as a receptionist to a Veterans Ministry case manager.

Hand up for men like old me.

Grace met my collapse. Scars linger, emptiness gone—purpose, faith, community filled it.

Still out there in your car or on your cell, "too far gone"? A door is open. Call Boise Rescue (208) 343-2389 or go to boiserm.org.

Rock bottom gave me time to face the man I became. I had chosen the bottle since Kitzingen.

Still stuck? Say at booking, "Veteran—flag VJO." They bring an application and a clean ride. Call Mission, boiserm.org, or 988 and press 1, now. One reach starts the climb.

Chapter 18

The "Girls" and Me

Graduation day, May 13, 2016, arrived under a Boise sky so clear it hurt to look at. The community hall smelled of fresh coffee, cut flowers wilting sweetly in vases, and the faint nervous sweat of men who still couldn't quite believe they belonged in dress shirts and ties. I stood on the stage, holding a crisp certificate, my hand trembling just enough for the paper to rustle. When Reverend Roscoe called my name, the room erupted, with handshakes, back slaps, and a few quiet sobs from brothers who'd walked in the same dark hallway with me. Pride surged so fiercely it burned behind my eyes, and aching joy followed close behind, tangled with the knowledge of how close I'd come to never standing there at all. I interned as an administrative assistant those final months, answering phones, sorting mail, and offering coffee to men whose eyes still carried the same hollow look I'd worn in the Walmart parking lot. Now I was hired full-time as a receptionist at the front desk, living upstairs in the staff quarters until 2021. Every "Welcome, brother" I spoke felt like repayment on a debt I could never fully settle.

Volunteering at the Idaho State Veterans Home filled my days off. The craft room smelled of glue sticks, acrylic paint, and the clean, earthy scent of old hands folding origami cranes. I helped mostly Vietnam vets, a few from Korea, paint wooden birdhouses, model airplanes, and small wooden crosses. Their fingers shook, and mine steadied them.

One afternoon, an older man with a Purple Heart tattooed on his forearm looked up from a half-finished B-17 and said, "You remind me of my boy before he shipped out." His voice cracked.

Mine did too when I answered, "I'm just glad to be here." Peace settled over me in those moments—the same reverence I'd felt casting flies on the Madison River at dusk, only now it was reverence for survival, for second chances, for men who carried invisible wounds and still showed up to paint.

That was where I met Janet.

She worked in Restorative Services. She had gentle hands, a steady voice, and golden hair pulled back behind her ears. I discreetly asked around first, terrified of misreading the situation. Then I gathered what courage I had left and asked her out for coffee after a shift. She said yes. A week later, I asked her to go on a motorcycle ride to McCall on our next day off. She said yes again.

We rode up the Payette River canyon on a late-summer afternoon. Wind roared past our helmets, sun flashed off water far below, and the Harley's engine thrummed steady beneath us. We pulled over at a gravel turnout above the river, with cottonwoods rustling, current murmuring secrets against stone. We took off helmets, sat on a fallen log, and opened our hearts without rehearsal.

She spoke first. Her son and daughter-in-law were both in the Air Force Reserve. He'd just returned from the Middle East. She described the strain of caring for elderly parents who lived with her, dealing with medications, doctor visits, and the slow erosion of independence. Stress lived in her voice, but did so fiercely. I listened, my chest tight with admiration for a woman who carried so much without breaking.

Then it was my turn. I told her everything—no polish, no omissions. Mission life and work. The wreckage of two marriages. Sons whom I'd failed so badly that their trust had dimmed. The drug and alcohol abuse that carved canyons throughout my life. Germany's first cracks. The farm raid. Incarcerations. Recovery. The jail cell where I'd finally run out of lies. My voice shook as shame burned hot behind my eyes. When I finished, silence stretched between us, the river murmuring, wind moving through leaves, my heart hammering so loud I was sure she could hear it.

She looked at me for a long time. Stood. Put her helmet back on, and said only two words. "That's a lot."

Then, "Let's ride."

We rode on. No promises. No assurances. Just the road, the engine's steady throb, her arms around my waist when we leaned into curves. Fear and confusion churned inside me—fear she'd disappear like the Montana girl, confusion that anyone could hear the worst and still stay. Yet beneath it, a faint, trembling hope stirred that maybe wreckage could be loved. Maybe broken could still be chosen.

We got married on July 15, 2021. Wanting to do it right this time, I proposed on one knee after a ride to see Shoshone Falls in central Idaho. She said yes. We waited a full year before the ceremony—engaged, deliberate, honoring the gravity of what we were stepping into. My New Life counselor, now a dear friend, officiated. When Janet walked toward me in simple yellow, eyes steady and bright, feelings of love surged so powerfully that they stole my breath. I vowed to cherish, to stay sober, to show up. She vowed to hold space for my scars, to ride beside me through whatever came. Rings slid on. We kissed. The room exhaled.

Then we climbed on "Lucy," my full-dress Harley, named for the clarity she brought, and rode north to McCall with a JUST MARRIED sign taped to the back, white streamers snapping in the wind. We laughed like teenagers, wind stripping years of weight from my shoulders. In a quiet pullout overlooking Payette Lake, we stopped, engines ticking down, and decided together that our memories from there on forward would be the adventures we built, not the wreckage behind us. Life was showing grace for my past. We held each other under stars reflecting on black water, her head on my chest, her heartbeat steady against mine. This woman had seen my worst and had still chosen me.

"Lucy" became more than transportation—she was wind therapy in upholstery and chrome. Janet's arms around my waist, the engine's deep thrum vibrating through our ribs, wind roaring past us, stripping heavy memories layer by layer. Sometimes we rode in silence—just the bike, our heartbeats, and the horizon. Curves and torque pulled us together, and her touch grounded me when old ghosts whispered.

In summer 2023, we headed north through the Sawtooth mountains to Stanley to stay with new friends of hers. We white-water rafted the Salmon River on the way, river spray cold on skin, laughter rising over roaring water. In 2024, we rode again to Lolo Pass into Montana, to Glacier National Park's jagged peaks, jet-boating Hells Canyon's churning brown water, soaking in Coeur d'Alene's cool lake. Each mile rebuilt inside me trust, joy, and the certainty that life could still hold beauty.

The year 2025 brought the long loop to Sturgis, North Dakota, over a thousand miles of northwest highways, Teton mountains rising sharply against the sky, Wyoming plains stretching endlessly, Black Hills rolling green and gold. Stops in Ammon, Riverton, and Jackson Hole, motel rooms smelling of pine cleaner, we had meals in diners and swapped rider stories over coffee. "Lucy" broke down in a gravel lot outside Jackson. The clutch basket hub nut backed out, threatening to strand us before Grand Teton Pass. Panic flared hot in me, but Janet's calm hand on my arm steadied me. We tore into the repair together, tools spread on gravel, her holding a flashlight while I worked, grease blackening both our hands. By late afternoon, we were rolling again, the hot July sun on our backs, relief sharp as the mountain air. We arrived in Sturgis the next day feeling like real-world adventurers, tent city humming around us, old-school rally chaos under an endless sky.

Mount Rushmore rose massively and silently. We stood

beneath those stone faces, wind tugging at our jackets, as quiet awe settled deep. Deadwood's historic streets carried the faint memory of Wild Bill Hickok's last poker hand. High winds in Wyoming whipped us sideways on the return, as thunderstorms in South Dakota pelted us with cold rain. We stayed rock-solid, engine thumping a steady rhythm, Janet's arms tight around me, rain streaming off helmets. "Lucy" carried us home, a dependable chariot, revival on two wheels, proof that broken could be fixed and still run true.

Today we live as one. I serve as the Senior Veterans Ministry Program case manager at the Mission, an advocate in Veterans Treatment Court, and Director of the American Legion Riders. Clean. Sober. My purpose is real. Janet's love embraces me steadily and for sure. My sons matter again. Through conversations and visits, trust is slowly rebuilding. My love for them burns brighter than ever, while the fear of losing them again still simmers beneath, a reminder to stay vigilant. But the dread no longer owns me. Confusion has given way to clarity. Awe arrives daily in a son's laugh, in Janet's hand in mine, in the rumble of "Lucy" beneath us.

The first ride after the river confession was grace after so many empty years. I laid my wreckage bare; she chose to stay and held on. "Lucy" is more than a bike. The thump of the engine, arms around the waist, wind stripping old noise. Breakdowns were fixed together in gravel lots. Once, I sat alone in a Walmart parking lot. Now, I ride two-up with a woman who chose truth, help brothers still in shadows, and live clean. Grace landed. Hard. Real.

If you think love and purpose feel reserved for the unbroken, know that shame lies. Janet saw the fighter beneath the wreckage and chose that version of me. We needed real, not perfect. Is your head loud? Use your tools: a meeting, a sponsor, or a long ride. Tell Janet. She'll listen. She always does.

Chapter 19

Relapse

Comfort had crept in so quietly that I never heard it open the door. Years into sobriety, the days felt solid. I had staff shifts at the Mission answering phones with steady hands, case-management sessions where broken men looked at me and saw possibility instead of judgment, American Legion Riders meetings where laughter rose over coffee and route maps, two-up rides with Janet on "Lucy" through Idaho's high passes, wind roaring past our helmets, her arms locked around my waist like an anchor I no longer feared losing. From the outside, life looked rebuilt, clean, purposeful, respected. Inside, I had let old thinking slip back through hairline cracks I pretended weren't there.

Marijuana was the first thread pulled. It arrived small and familiar—the same gateway drug I'd first touched behind the barn in high school, the same sweet smoke that had quieted barracks nights in Germany. I had just a little after long days of holding space for other men's pain. I told myself it wasn't serious. I wasn't drinking. I wasn't chasing meth or pills. It was only weed—soft, harmless, a way to soften edges when the stories hit too close to my own buried wounds. Rationalization came easily. *You've earned a little slack after everything.* The lie was satisfying at first, like the first drag after years of fighting the urge.

Then guilt arrived—swift, scalding, familiar as an old scar reopening. I'd catch myself staring at Janet across the kitchen table, lamplight catching silver in her hair, her quiet strength, the only thing that had ever held me when the floor dropped out. Shame twisted like a blade. What would she see if she knew? The man who'd finally stood up, or the one sliding back into the same hole he'd crawled out of. Fear felt hot behind my eyes—fear of losing her, fear that one poor choice could erase the decade we'd built together. My love for her burned fiercer than ever. The thought of breaking her trust again left me nauseous, chest tight, breath shallow.

Worse still was the dread of the Mission. I wasn't just a graduate anymore. I was staff, a case manager, a face new men looked to when they walked through the doors, hollow-eyed and ashamed. What would Reverend Roscoe, the man who'd given me a second, third, fourth chance without ever asking me to deserve it, say? What would the brothers, the ones who still called me "Sarge" with quiet respect, think if they learned their guide had slipped? I pictured the conversations full of disappointed glances, trust quietly withdrawn, the possibility of being asked to leave. The job wasn't about income; it was daily redemption. Every intake, every handshake, every "you're not alone" I spoke was proof I'd come back from the Walmart parking lot. Losing that would feel like erasing the man I'd fought to become.

Nights grew restless. I'd wake at 0300, heart racing, staring at the ceiling fan's slow blades while Janet slept beside me, her breathing steady and trusting. The old insomnia returned—not the bone-deep exhaustion of basic training, but something colder, sharper. Dread sat heavy in my chest like wet concrete. Confusion choked every thought. How could I have let this happen again, after workbooks, after accountability partners, after every tool, I'd sworn to keep sharp? The lie whispered louder. *It's not the hard stuff. It's just weed. You're still better than before.* I hated the voice. I hated myself for listening.

The random urine analysis (UA) came on a Tuesday morning, standard staff protocol, nothing personal. I knew what it would show the moment the cup was handed to me. My stomach dropped through the floor. No excuses left. No place to hide. I walked straight to my supervisor's office, palms slick, voice barely steady enough to form words. "I need to talk to you. I slipped. Marijuana. I'm sorry. I'm wrong. I need help getting back on track."

The words hung in the small office like smoke after a fire. I braced for termination, for the end of everything I'd rebuilt, for the confirmation that I was still the man who always fell. Instead, grace landed again—grace I hadn't earned, grace I still don't fully understand. After long hours of prayer, after conversations with leadership that left me raw and exposed, they chose not to let me go. They required renewed counseling, weekly check-ins, and renewed accountability. There was no public announcement. No shame. Just firm, steady mercy.

That night, I sat at the kitchen table after Janet had gone to bed, the workbook open under a single bulb. Pages felt heavier that time, ink-stained from earlier rounds, corners dog-eared from nights I'd wept over them. The process forced me to name the old lie again, the one rooted so deep I'd stopped hearing it as foreign: *You're not enough. You never were. Numb it, or you'll fall apart.* It had started in Alabama under the weight of being watched, carried through Idaho schools as the PK who had to reflect well, followed me into Germany, where belonging became risk, survived the farm raid and jail cell, only to whisper again now: *One more time won't hurt. You've already proven you're broken.*

I mapped out the "Deja Vu" cycles on fresh pages. Arrows between words, showing how "isolation after tough case days" led to "secrecy" led to "small compromises" led to "shame" and had me "return to old medicine." The FASTER Relapse Awareness Scale became my daily mirror:

- **Fantasy:** Picturing the high.
- **Anxiety:** What if they find out?
- **Self-pity:** "I've earned this."
- **Tension:** Chest tight, jaw clenched.

- **Excitement:** The anticipation.

- **Rationalization:** "It's not really using."

I scored high on every point without realizing how far I'd drifted. Naming them out loud—first on paper, then in counseling—stripped their power. They weren't mysterious forces. They were old, familiar lies I could finally challenge.

I told Janet everything that same night, no minimizing, no half-truths. She listened, eyes steady, hands folded in her lap. When I finished, she didn't speak for a long moment. Then she reached across the table, took both my hands in hers, and said, "We fix this together. But no more secrets. Ever." Her trust hurt more than anger would have. It reminded me what was at stake—her love, our life, the fragile miracle we'd built. Protective love surged inside me so fiercely I could barely breathe. I would not lose her. Not to my own cowardice.

My body still carries the scars, with nightmares that wake me gasping at odd hours, my stomach burning when stress rises, memory gaps from decades of abuse, and an introversion that makes crowds feel like enemy territory. But the Mission remained a safe harbor. I stayed on staff. I kept showing up—raw, humbled, accountable—clean and sober one honest day at a time.

Comfort had nearly killed me once by convincing me the fight was over. Old thinking waits for exhaustion, for pride, for a moment when you believe you've earned a pass. For me, it wore marijuana's soft face of—"just a little," or "not the hard stuff." Same lie, new wrapper.

The UA forced truth into daylight. Confession burned. I expected to lose everything— Janet, the job, the trust

I'd rebuilt brick by brick. Instead, grace arrived again in prayer, counseling, and a reset. The workbook named the lie: *You're not enough—numb it.* Roots ran deep in me, as a watched PK, a soldier who crossed lines, a dad who failed his boys. Cycles mapped. The FASTER scale caught my drift early. Humility returned, sharp and necessary. Accountabilities rebuilt what secrecy had eroded.

Slips test you, but they don't define you. Has old thinking returned? Don't hide. Confess to someone who won't bullshit you. Grab the tools that worked before— a meeting, a sponsor—and own the lie with fresh humility. You've got experience now. The next hour matters to confess, return to the circle, and work the steps again.

Grace shows up new every morning. The crew is still there—Janet, the Mission brothers, the Riders. I reached out. She held on. Leadership gave me room to grow. You can too. One confession reset me. One call, one meeting, one honest prayer can reset you.

Keep moving. Hold on. Tell someone. The river keeps flowing. So can you.

Buddy Note

Comfort sneaks in when you think the fight's over. Brother, If you're reading this, you may be carrying more pain than you let on. I've been there. For a long time, I believed I was too far gone to ever change. I was wrong. The turning point came when

I stopped trying to do it alone and started reaching out for help. That one decision changed everything. You don't have to have it all figured out. You just need to take the next right step — no matter how small. And once you start getting better, look for ways to help the next guy coming behind you. That's how we stay free. You are not alone. Help is available, and there's still a life worth living on the other side of where you are right now. Keep moving forward. One day at a time.

PART IV

Legacy

CHAPTER 20

THE "RIDERS" AND SERVICE

The American Legion Riders became more than a hobby—they were my lifeline, a roaring testament to the recovery that had pulled me from the abyss. Founded in 1993 as a program of The American Legion, the Riders are a nationwide motorcycle association dedicated to serving veterans, their families, and communities through patriotism, charity, and camaraderie. With over 110,000 members across chapters in every state, they raise millions annually for causes like veteran suicide prevention, homeless veteran support, and scholarships for children of fallen service members. It's not just about the bikes; it's about honoring the oath we took and extending that service beyond active duty into civilian life. For me, joining Post 113 in Boise after graduating from the New Life Program in 2016 felt like rediscovering the crew bonds I'd known in the Army—brothers and sisters united not by tanks, but by chrome, leather, and a shared commitment to never leave a comrade behind.

As Director of the Riders chapter, I threw myself into planning and leading events, each one a step further from the isolation that had nearly destroyed me. The role demanded responsibility, coordinating routes, securing permits, and rallying volunteers, but it also offered redemption. Where once my hands had shaken from withdrawal or gripped a bottle in despair, now they steadied handlebars or shook the hands of grateful veterans. The shame that had silenced me for years began to crack under the weight of purpose, as every mile ridden and every dollar raised was a quiet victory over the man I'd been in that Walmart parking lot. Recovery wasn't just sobriety—it was reclaiming my voice, my strength, and my place in a community that saw me not as a failure, but as a survivor ready to lead.

Patriot Thunder stood as the crown jewel of our efforts, an annual spectacle that embodied the power of collective healing. Organized by the Idaho American Legion Riders, this massive ride draws over 1,200 motorcycles from across the state and beyond, converging in a thunderous tribute to fallen heroes and living veterans. It began in 2005 as a small memorial event but has grown into a flagship fundraiser, supporting initiatives such as the Idaho Veterans Assistance League and local VA programs.

The ride typically spans 100 to 150 miles through Idaho's stunning landscapes, winding canyons, open plains, and mountain passes, culminating in ceremonies at veterans' memorials or cemeteries. Funds raised, often exceeding $50,000, go toward adaptive equipment for disabled vets, emergency aid for homeless service members, and youth programs that instill the values we fought for.

For me, Patriot Thunder was pure emotional alchemy, transforming the pain of my past into something profound and shared. The event kicked off at dawn in a vast parking lot at Expo Idaho, the air thick with the sharp tang of gasoline, dew-damp leather jackets, and the faint metallic bite of engines warming up. As riders gathered, leather vests adorned with patches from Vietnam, Desert Storm, Afghanistan, conversations flowed like old war stories, with quiet nods of recognition, slaps on the back, eyes meeting with unspoken understanding. I stood among them, hearts swollen with a gratitude that often brought tears to my eyes. Just years earlier, I'd been alone in a jail cell, convinced I was beyond saving. Now, as Director, I helped orchestrate this symphony of solidarity.

When the signal came, engines coughed to life one by one, building into a deafening roar that vibrated through my bones and chest like a living pulse, shaking loose the remnants of despair. We rolled out in tight formation, a serpentine column of gleaming chrome stretching for miles, flags whipping in the wind like battle standards. The ground trembled under the collective weight of Harleys, Indians, and Hondas, exhaust clouds billowing gray and acrid, mixing with the earthy scent of valley soil kicked up by tires. Wind whipped against my face, helmet buzzing with the hum of intercom chatter, jokes to lighten the mood, route calls for safety, and quiet affirmations of

"We've got your back." As we snaked through sun-dappled canyons and vast open plains, horns blasted in unison at roadside memorials, a wave of sound that echoed off the hills, honoring those who served and sacrificed. The sheer thunderous volume of it drowned out the inner demons that still whispered in quiet moments, replacing them with a profound sense of belonging.

One year, during a particularly grueling stretch through high winds and sudden rain, I felt the old pull of doubt creep in—the familiar ache of wondering if I deserved this second chance. But Janet, riding pillion on "Lucy," squeezed my waist, her presence as always an anchor. We pulled over at a veterans' cemetery stop, rain dripping from our helmets as we stood in silent vigil, hands over hearts. A young widow approached, tears in her eyes, thanking us for remembering her husband, lost in Afghanistan. In that moment, handing her a check from our funds, emotion surged through me like a cleansing flood—grief for my own losses mingled with joy at being part of something greater. Patriot Thunder wasn't just "a ride." It was therapy on two wheels, the collective thunder forging bonds that healed wounds I thought were permanent. It reminded me that recovery is ongoing, fueled by service, and that every rev of the throttle was a promise to myself and others that we rise together.

Beyond Patriot Thunder, the Riders' calendar brimmed with events that deepened the emotional layers of my recovery. The Frank Smith Memorial Ride, named for a fallen local hero, started with somber meetings in the Legion Hall, coffee steaming in Styrofoam cups as voices overlapped with ideas for routes and tributes. Quilts of Valor presentations at Expo Idaho were intimate affairs, fabric soft and warm under my hands as we draped handmade quilts over veterans' shoulders, their eyes shining with unshed tears, mirroring the vulnerability I'd learned to embrace in group sessions. The Veterans Day Parade in Boise brought crowds lining the streets, flags snapping in the wind behind our bikes, engines rumbling low and steady as applause washed over us like a balm.

The Sheriffs' Association speech in 2017 marked another emotional milestone, a full-circle moment that amplified my recovery's depth. Standing at the podium in a room smelling of coffee and the buffet breakfast, faces attentive and expectant, I shared my life's jagged arc—the Army in the 70s, the National Guard with the 116th, the depths of alcoholism that led to that fateful Walmart DUI. My voice steadied as I asked and urged, "Booking someone who served? Alert VJO." The applause that followed wasn't just approval; it was affirmation that my broken path had value, that vulnerability could inspire change. In that room, I felt the weight of shame lift further, replaced by the quiet pride of advocacy.

Buddy Note

Legion Riders became a lifeline, a crew reborn in chrome and leather with over 110,000 members raising millions for vets: suicide prevention, homeless aid, scholarships. Not just bikes, but patriotism, charity, and never leaving a brother behind. I joined Post 113 Boise in 2016. I felt turret trust again. As Director, I planned routes and rallies. My hands that once shook from withdrawal now steadied handlebars, shook grateful vets. Shame cracked under purpose. Every mile and dollar was a win over Walmart-lot man.

Patriot Thunder is over 1,200 bikes thundering at dawn from Expo Idaho. The roar shook the chest like an old diesel. Miles-long column, flags whipping, horns blasting, memorials. Drowned demons built belonging.

During a stormy ride, doubt crept. But Janet squeezed me on "Lucy." Cemetery stops in the rain; the widow, in tears, thanked us. Handing her a check, grief and joy collided. Therapy on wheels.

Events deepened healing. Frank Smith Memorial. Quilts of Valor, filled with warm fabric and shining eyes. Veterans Day Parade with crowds and rumbling applause. The 2017 Sheriffs' Association speech, when I shared my arc, asked and urged, "Booking vet? Alert VJO." Applause gave a broken path value.

My legacy was showing up daily, mile after mile. Handshakes, rides for the fallen, speeches reaching just one in the shadows. My choice to be sober, serve, and tell my story unflinchingly. Shame whispers faintly. Hope, like a jail spark, a steady flame via Riders and road. Healing one ride, one act. I found life worth living. I never planned to write a book—just to speak the truth. Are you riding solo, inside your head, with a train in the distance? Isolation whispers, Too broken to belong. The lie kept me in the lot, the cell, the cab. Be patient.

Riders, Mission, Legion, and Vet Centers are full of people who have ridden in the dark. Need presence, not perfection. One "vet struggling" at the meeting, one Riders call, one guest ride cracks the door open.

The oath is to leave no one behind, including the one in the mirror. Grab the handlebars. Find a crew, one ride, one handshake.

Chapter 21

In Retrospect

The river never stopped flowing.

It moved quietly and patiently through Emmett's willow bottoms when I was small, carrying silt and small wonders while I watched a red-and-white bobber dance in the current. That same river—steady, indifferent, merciful—still carves its path today through Idaho basalt, never hurrying, never asking permission. It carried secrets then, and now it carries memory. And somehow, against every expectation, it carried me through every bend and fall.

Looking back, the arc is no longer made up of fragments. It is one continuous current. Mornings heavy with honeysuckle and certainty at the Alabama parsonage. Dad's footsteps pacing after midnight threats, justice resting on young shoulders. Idaho gravel banks where silence first became sanctuary. High school keggers where I tasted both thrill and guilt. Fort Knox gravel under boots, the sharp crack of an M16, the deep diesel pulse of an M60A1 that briefly made me feel large enough to matter. Kitzingen's sloppy snow winters. Gasthaus beer, hash curling against concrete ceilings, and the two heroin chases I barely escaped. The Article 15 that should have been a siren but became only the first deep fracture.

Then the long slide of Portland docks and first marriage fraying, a newborn son's fist curling around my finger with a promise I could not keep. Heyburn farm illusion with pheasants strutting under open sky, hidden grow lights humming behind false walls, dawn cruisers boiling dust in the mirror. Trucking blackouts on high passes, Ambien chased with whiskey, twenty unaccounted miles, wondering who I might have killed. Twin Falls Walmart parking lot, a half-gallon beside me like a faithful but deadly companion, red-and-blue lights strobing through cracked glass, 197 days on thin mats breathing bleach and regret, hallway light slicing concrete like a thin, patient promise.

And then mercy—unearned, stubborn, arriving precisely when I had nothing left to trade—VJO reaching into that cell. New Life doors opening to coffee, clean sheets, and brothers who nodded instead of turning away. Janet's arms around my waist on "Lucy," wind peeling decades of noise away one layer at a time. Patriot Thunder's roar, shaking loose the last echoes of isolation. Sons' voices returning on the phone, trust mending slowly and real. A life not flawless, but present.

I am thankful beyond what words can convey.

Thankful for river bottoms that taught stillness when the world demanded performance. Thankful for the Army that gave noise loud enough to quiet the silence for a season, crew bonds fierce enough to show what trust could be. Thankful for every fracture—Germany hash, farm raid, trucking voids—because each one, painfully, hollowed space where grace could finally enter. Thankful for Judge Harris naming me "stubborn but smart," for VJO throwing the rope, for Reverend Roscoe and Mission brothers who refused to let me vanish. Thankful for Janet, who heard about the wreckage and still said, "Let's ride." Thankful for "Lucy's" steady thump beneath us, for wind therapy that clears what language cannot reach. Thankful for every Patriot Thunder mile, every Quilt of Valor draped over trembling shoulders, every handshake at the Veterans Home craft table, every new man who walks through Mission doors and sees in me not ruin, but evidence that the climb is possible.

Above all, I am thankful for my sons, who remained my deepest reason, even when I gave them every reason to walk away. You stood by me through nights I no longer knew how to stand on my own. Your quiet strength—your refusal to let shame write the final line—kept a small flame burning when I could not see it. I failed you in ways that still ache in the quiet hours. Yet here we are with conversations again, visits, trust rebuilding like riverbank soil after a flood. I do not deserve the mercy of still being called your dad. But I will spend every remaining sunrise earning the right to try.

This path was never about dramatic singularity. Far too many veterans carry the same unseen wounds—the structure ends, old habits rush to fill the void, isolation creeps, fractures widen into canyons. This story is ordinary in its pain, extraordinary only in its mercy. Collapse is never the final chapter, but the pivot that demands the turn. The rise does not arrive in a single blaze. It arrives one honest confession, one extended hand, one sober dawn at a time.

If you are reading these words from the shadows, on a cell, porch, or barracks cot, or in a car or truck-stop sleeper—you are not beyond reach. The river still runs. Grace still finds cracks. The same stubborn spark in me that refused bail in Twin Falls, that kept scratching truth onto paper under jail fluorescents, that climbed back onto "Lucy" after every fall, is alive in you too. Shame feels permanent only because it has held the microphone too long. Take it back. Speak the quiet part aloud—to a battle buddy, a sponsor, a partner or spouse who listens steadily, a VJO specialist. Call 988 and press 1. One sentence. One reach. That is enough to begin.

These pages exist not to glorify the dark, but to place one small lantern along the overgrown trail, not because my story is exceptional, but because it is shared. If even one brother still walking that rough road reads these words and thinks, *If he came back, maybe I can too*, then every mile, every tear, every blackout is redeemed.

The river taught patience. Recovery taught speaking. Service taught purpose. Janet taught me I could still be chosen. The Riders taught me we rise together.

And God—quiet, patient, relentlessly merciful—taught me I was never truly alone.

I am here. Clean. Sober. Present. Thankful. Still healing, still riding, and still reaching back.

The current keeps moving. So can you.

Hold on. Tell someone. The rise is closer than it feels.

Buddy Note

Collapse wasn't the end; it was a pivot. Rise isn't instant—it's one confession, one hand reaching out, one sober sunrise. If you're in shadows right now, in a car, on a cell, on a porch, in a sleeper berth, shame's loud because it's held mic too long. Take it back. Say five words at booking or court: "I'm a veteran—flag VJO." Or call 988 and press 1, Boise Rescue (208) 343-2389, or a sober Legion vet. One reach starts the current again. You're not too far gone. The river still flows. Grace still finds cracks. Hold one more dawn. Tell someone you served. We're still out here—no one left behind.

APPENDICES

Appendix A

M60A1

Appendix A provides essential historical context for the M60A1 tank, the armored vehicle I crewed as a gunner during my service in Germany with the 3rd Infantry Division in the mid-1970s. This main battle tank was a cornerstone of U.S. armored forces during the Cold War, particularly in NATO's forward-deployed units along the Inner German Border.

Historical Background, Development, and Production: Evolved as an upgrade from the M48 Patton series. Approved in 1960, the M60A1 featured a redesigned turret (longer, wider, more spacious internally) with improved ballistic protection, better crew ergonomics, and a new gun mount. Production ran from 1962 to 1980 at Detroit Arsenal Tank Plant (Chrysler and General Dynamics), with approximately 7,948 built (part of over 15,000 total M60-family tanks).

Cold War Role: Deployed extensively in NATO's Central Army Group, particularly in West Germany (e.g., units like 1st Armored Division, 3rd Armored Division, armored cavalry regiments). It was central to defending key invasion corridors, such as the Fulda Gap, a lowland route through Hesse and Thuringia where Warsaw Pact forces (the Soviet 8th Guards Army, etc.) were expected to thrust toward the Rhine if war erupted. M60A1-equipped units conducted constant alerts, border patrols, Return of Forces to Germany (REFORGER) exercises, and live-fire drills to deter or delay a Soviet armored breakthrough.

Legacy: Phased out in US service by the 1990s (many upgraded to M60A3 or retired), but exported widely and used by allies into the 2000s to 2010s. Known for reliability, firepower, and crew survivability compared to contemporaries like the T-62 or the T-7.

Appendix B

New Life Program at Boise Rescue Mission Ministries

The New Life Discipleship and Recovery Program is Boise Rescue Mission Ministries' long-term, faith-based addiction recovery program for men and women struggling with substance abuse. Since its beginning in 1996, the program has helped more than 400 participants gain the tools they need to stay addiction-free and become Christ-centered, self-sufficient members of the community.

PROGRAM OVERVIEW

- **Length:** Twelve to twenty-four months (typically twelve months for men at River of Life; longer options available).

- **Structure:** Year-long (or extended) in-house discipleship and recovery combining spiritual, mental, and physical elements.

- **Spiritual:** Biblical teachings, daily Bible study, prayer, devotions, chapel services, and spiritual formation offered without coercion. Focus on filling the emptiness left by addiction with faith and grace.

- **Mental:** Trauma-informed counseling (individual and group), relapse prevention, addressing PTSD, isolation, and addictive behaviors.

- **Physical and Life Skills:** Work readiness, financial accountability, daily routine, peer support, life-skills training (job search, budgeting, responsibility).

- **Capacity:** Men's Program at River of Life—forty-two participants (includes candidate and probationary stage).

- **Approach:** Not just abstinence, but holistic discipleship and accountability to build long-term sobriety, integrity, and community reintegration. No force on faith; participants engage at their own pace.

- **Eligibility:** Adults (men at River of Life) experiencing life-altering substance abuse problems. Must be willing to commit to structure, honesty, and participation.

- **Candidate Stage:** Thirty-day probationary period to assess fit for the program and allow the Mission to determine appropriateness.

- **Application Process:** Contact the Boise Rescue Mission (River of Life for men). Call (208) 343-2389 or visit boiserm.org to request an application. Complete and submit the New Life Program Application (available as a PDF on boiserm.org or through staff). Include personal info, history, and why you want to join, as well as an interview and assessment. Staff review applications, conduct interviews, and determine if the program is a good fit.

- **Acceptance:** If approved, enter the program (often with immediate placement at River of Life shelter).

- **Policies:** Participants agree with rules (e.g., no substances, full participation, accountability). Full policies provided upon application.

  - **Contact Information:**
    - ▹ Boise Rescue Mission Ministries: boiserm.org
    - ▹ River of Life Shelter (Men): (208) 343-2389

  - **Application PDF:** Available at boiserm.org/wp-content/uploads/2025/02/NLP-Application.pdf (or search site for latest).

  - **Program Description PDF:** boiserm.org/wp-content/uploads/2025/02/NLP-Program-Description.pdf.

This program changed my life—it can change yours too. If you're a veteran or know one in need, reach out. The door is open.

Appendix C

VA Hotline and VJO Quick References

IMMEDIATE HELP FOR VETERANS IN CRISIS

If you're in danger or struggling right now, use these resources. One call can change everything.

NATIONAL VETERANS CRISIS LINE

- Call or text 988, then press 1 or dial (1-800) 273-8255 and press 1.
- Chat online at veteranscrisisline.net.
- 24/7 confidential support for veterans, service members, and their families.
- Covers suicide prevention, post-traumatic stress disorder (PTSD), substance abuse, homelessness, military sexual trauma, and more.

- You can expect trained responders who listen, connect you to local VA resources, and help with immediate safety.

- **Veterans Justice Outreach (VJO)**

- **Purpose:** Helps justice-involved veterans (jail, court, probation) access VA services and treatment instead of just punishment.

- **What To Do:** When booking or at court, say "I'm a veteran" or ask for the veteran flag on your booking record. This alerts the VJO specialist in your area.

- **Idaho Regions:** The state is divided into four regions. Contact your local VA or call 988 and press 1 for a VJO referral.

- **More Information:** va.gov/homeless/vjo.asp or ask jail staff or the court to connect you.

- **Quick Tip:** If you're in jail or court, say, "I'm a veteran, please alert VJO." It can open doors to treatment programs like New Life instead of longer sentences.

Appendix D

Key Veteran Readjustment and Transition Resources (2026)

The military-to-civilian transition can feel like losing structure overnight. These resources help bridge that gap. Many are free, confidential, and veteran-focused. Reach out early. The earlier you connect, the smoother the road.

TRANSITION ASSISTANCE PROGRAM (TAP)

Mandatory Department of Defense (DOD) or VA program for separating service members (active, Guard, Reserve). Includes in-person or virtual workshops on VA benefits, employment, education, health, and reintegration. Covers resume building, job search, disability claims, and family support.

Start Here: tapevents.mil or contact your base or installation transition office. The VA Benefits and Services course explains health care, compensation, career readiness, housing, and community connections.

VA TAP Page: www.benefits.va.gov/transition/tap.asp

VET CENTERS (READJUSTMENT COUNSELING)

Confidential, no-cost counseling in relaxed community settings (non-medical). Specializing in post-deployment readjustment, PTSD, MST, family issues, bereavement, and substance use. Open to all eras, including families. Find the nearest VA center at vetcenter.va.gov or call 877-WAR-VETS (927-8387). Idaho locations include Boise, Twin Falls, and outreach sites.

VETERAN READINESS AND EMPLOYMENT (VR&E)

VA program for job training, resume help, education, employment accommodations, and self-employment support if service-connected disability affects work. Includes counseling and tools for civilian career transition.

Apply: benefits.va.gov/vocrehab

MILITARY ONESOURCE

Provides 24/7 support for transitioning veterans and families. Consultants help with reintegration, relocation, employment, finances, and mental health referrals. Includes post-deployment guides and spouse transition tools.

Call: 1-800-342-9647

Go To: militaryonesource.mil/transition-retirement

IDAHO-SPECIFIC TRANSITION SUPPORT

Idaho Division of Veterans Services (IDVS) provides state benefits navigation, education or training, employment help, and homeless veteran assistance. Transition Assistance Advisors (TAAs) in regions. E.g., Central Idaho: Angel Smith, (202) 987-3877, or Eastern Idaho: Hayley Rienstra, (202) 987-3906 at idvs.idaho.gov. Boise VA Medical Center and Vet Centers for local readjustment counseling, health care, and benefits claims (va.gov/boise-healthcare).

OTHER NATIONAL TRANSITION PROGRAMS

- **Commit Foundation:** High-touch mentoring, workshops, and executive coaching for purpose-driven careers at commitfoundation.org. SkillBridge (DOD), up to 180 days of civilian job training or internships before separation.

- **Veterans Crisis Line:** Immediate support (mental health, substance use, crisis). Call 988 then press 1 (24/7). If you're in crisis or struggling, call 988 and press 1 or text 838255. One call can connect you to local help fast. These resources saved lives, including mine, through VJO and New Life. Don't wait for the cracks to widen; reach out before the drift takes hold.

Appendix E

Recommended Reading and Resources

These books and tools helped me or others in recovery. They're practical, honest, and focus on veteran experiences, trauma, addiction, and rebuilding.

BOOKS

1. *The Body Keeps the Score* **by Bessel van der Kolk**: Explains how trauma (including military trauma) affects the body and mind, with healing tools.

2. *Unbroken* **by Laura Hillenbrand**: True story of resilience, survival, and redemption (World War II vet Louis Zamperini).

3. *Once a Warrior—Always a Warrior* **by Charles W. Hoge**: PTSD and reintegration for vets, a practical, no-nonsense guide.

4. *The Big Book of Alcoholics Anonymous* (AA): Classic for understanding alcoholism and recovery steps, free online at aa.org.

OTHER RESOURCES

- VA.gov: Free counseling, health care, housing, benefits for vets.
- 988 Veterans Crisis Line: Press 1 for 24/7 support.
- 2025 VA Federal Benefits Guide for Veterans, Dependents, Survivors, and Caregivers.
- 2025–2026 Veterans Benefits Manual (National Veterans Legal Services Program—NVLSP).
- VA Supportive Services for Veteran Families (SSVF) Program Guide (2025–2026 Edition).
- Boise Rescue Mission (boiserm.org): New Life Program and shelter.
- American Legion Riders: Local chapter rides and brotherhood.
- AA or NA Meetings: Find local groups at aa.org or na.org.

Appendix F

Accessibility of Veterans Resources for the Homeless Population in Boise

Homelessness among veterans remains a persistent and complex challenge across the United States, with Boise, Idaho, reflecting both the national trends and unique local dynamics. Veterans experiencing homelessness in Boise face a confluence of barriers, including limited affordable housing, mental health and substance use disorders, and difficulties navigating the web of available resources. This report provides a comprehensive analysis of the accessibility, reach, and effectiveness of veterans' resources for the homeless population in Boise, Idaho. It examines the availability and capacity of services such as housing assistance, mental health care, substance abuse treatment, employment support, and VA benefits navigation. The report also explores the roles of local governmental and nonprofit organizations, identifies key barriers to access, reviews recent policy changes, and evaluates outcomes and best practices. All claims and data are supported by current, credible sources, with detailed analysis following each summary table or list.

OVERVIEW OF HOMELESS VETERANS IN BOISE: PREVALENCE AND DEMOGRAPHICS

CURRENT STATISTICS AND TRENDS

Boise, as the largest city in Idaho and the seat of Ada County, serves as a focal point for veterans' services in the state. According to the 2025 Point-in-Time (PIT) Count conducted by Our Path Home, 772 individuals were experiencing homelessness in Ada County on the night of January 19, 2025, a 2 percent decrease from the previous year. While the PIT Count does not disaggregate all data by veteran status, national estimates and local program data suggest that veterans comprise approximately 8 to 11 percent of the adult homeless population in Boise, consistent with national averages.

Demographically, the majority of homeless veterans in Boise are male, with a significant proportion being Vietnam-era veterans, though the share of Gulf War and post-9/11 veterans is increasing. The Boise Rescue Mission Ministries' Veterans Ministry Program (VMP) reports that the typical participant is from the Vietnam era, with an average program stay of less than twelve months. Over 660 veterans have successfully transitioned from homelessness to independence through this program since its inception in 2010.

Nationally, veteran homelessness is characterized by high rates of chronic homelessness, mental health disorders, substance use issues, and physical disabilities. In Boise, these trends are mirrored, with local providers noting a high prevalence of co-occurring disorders and complex needs among their veteran clients.

KEY DEMOGRAPHIC INSIGHTS FROM THE 2025 POINT-IN-TIME (PIT) COUNT

- **Gender:** Nearly 90 percent of homeless veterans are men, though services for women veterans are expanding.

- **Age:** The majority are aged fifty and above, but younger veterans are increasingly represented.

- **Race and Ethnicity:** The veteran homeless population is predominantly white, but there is an overrepresentation of Native American and African American veterans relative to their share of the general population.

- **Service Era:** Vietnam-era veterans remain the largest cohort, but Gulf War and post-9/11 veterans are a growing segment.

- **Chronicity:** A significant portion of homeless veterans in Boise experience chronic homelessness, defined as long-term or repeated episodes of homelessness coupled with a disabling condition.

These demographic patterns inform the design and targeting of local services, as older veterans may require different supports than younger, recently discharged individuals.

VA BOISE HOMELESS VETERAN PROGRAMS: SERVICES AND CAPACITY

CORE VA PROGRAMS AND POINTS OF ACCESS

The Boise VA Medical Center (VAMC) is the primary federal provider of health and social services for homeless veterans in the region. The VA's Health Care for Homeless Veterans (HCHV) program, coordinated by dedicated care coordinators, serves as the main entry point for veterans experiencing or at risk of homelessness. Veterans can connect with care coordinators for immediate assistance with food, shelter, housing, job training, life skills, addiction treatment, and mental health care.

PROGRAM OR SERVICE	DESCRIPTION	CAPACITY AND NOTES
HCHV	OUTREACH, ASSESSMENT, CASE MANAGEMENT, AND REFERRAL TO VA AND COMMUNITY RESOURCES	MULTIPLE CARE COORDINATORS; CAPACITY VARIES
HUD-VASH (VA SUPPORTIVE HOUSING)	PERMANENT SUPPORTIVE HOUSING WITH RENTAL ASSISTANCE AND CASE MANAGEMENT	VARIES; SEE HOUSING SECTION FOR DETAILS
GRANT AND PER DIEM (GPD)	TRANSITIONAL HOUSING WITH SUPPORTIVE SERVICES	LIMITED BEDS; SEE HOUSING SECTION
SUBSTANCE ABUSE RESIDENTIAL REHABILITATION TREATMENT (SARRTP)	RESIDENTIAL ADDICTION TREATMENT FOR VETERANS	4 BEDS AT BOISE RESCUE MISSION; MORE AT VAMC
VA MENTAL HEALTH SERVICES	INPATIENT, OUTPATIENT, AND TELEHEALTH BEHAVIORAL HEALTH CARE	REGIONAL CENTER OF EXCELLENCE
VA REGIONAL BENEFIT OFFICE	BENEFITS NAVIGATION, CLAIMS ASSISTANCE, AND EMPLOYMENT SUPPORT	WALK-IN AND APPOINTMENT-BASED SERVICES

Table 1: Key VA Boise Homeless Veteran Programs

The VA Boise system is recognized as a regional center of excellence for veteran-focused mental health care, offering both inpatient and outpatient services, including telehealth options for rural veterans. The VA also provides substance use disorder treatment, job training, and support for justice-involved veterans.

CAPACITY AND REACH

While the VA offers a comprehensive suite of services, capacity constraints are a recurring challenge. For example, the number of HUD-VASH vouchers and GPD beds is limited, and waitlists can develop during periods of high demand. The VA's ability to provide same-day access to interim housing is contingent on bed availability, and recent federal staffing reductions have raised concerns about the sustainability of service levels.

The VA's Homeless Veteran Care team works closely with community partners to maximize reach. But some veterans remain outside the system due to eligibility issues, lack of awareness, or personal barriers.

LOCAL GOVERNMENTAL ORGANIZATIONS AND PROGRAMS

CITY, COUNTY, AND STATE INITIATIVES

Boise's response to veteran homelessness is shaped by a collaborative network involving city, county, and state agencies. The City of Boise, through its Innovation + Performance Housing Data Portal and participation in the Our Path Home partnership, plays a central role in data collection, policy development, and service coordination.

Ada County supports treatment and housing initiatives through its approved provider network, while the Idaho Division of Veterans Services (IDVS) oversees statewide programs and connects veterans to federal and local resources.

ORGANIZATION OR PROGRAM	ROLE OR SERVICES PROVIDED	CONTACT AND NOTES
CITY OF BOISE (OUR PATH HOME)	LEAD AGENCY FOR CONTINUUM OF CARE (COC); COORDINATES PIT COUNT, HOUSING PROGRAMS, AND SERVICE INTEGRATION	WWW.OURPATHHOME.ORG
ADA COUNTY	APPROVES TREATMENT PROVIDERS FOR SUBSTANCE USE AND MENTAL HEALTH; SUPPORTS HOUSING INITIATIVES	PROVIDER LIST UPDATED REGULARLY
IDVS	STATEWIDE BENEFITS NAVIGATION, OUTREACH, AND PROGRAM OVERSIGHT	WWW.VETERANS.IDAHO.GOV
IDAHO HOUSING AND FINANCE ASSOCIATION	ADMINISTERS FEDERAL HOMELESSNESS ASSISTANCE FUNDS, RAPID REHOUSING, AND PERMANENT SUPPORTIVE HOUSING	WWW.IDAHOHOUSING.COM

Table 2: Governmental Organizations and Programs

These agencies work in tandem with the VA and non-profit partners to deliver a coordinated response, though gaps in communication and resource allocation persist.

NONPROFIT ORGANIZATIONS SERVING HOMELESS VETERANS IN BOISE

MAJOR NONPROFIT PROVIDERS

Nonprofit organizations are critical to Boise's homeless veteran services landscape, often filling gaps left by governmental programs and providing flexible, low-barrier support.

ORGANIZATION	SERVICES OFFERED	CAPACITY AND IMPACT
BOISE RESCUE MISSION MINISTRIES (BRMM)	VETERANS MINISTRY PROGRAM (VMP) FOR TRANSITIONAL HOUSING, CASE, MANAGEMENT, FOOD, COUNSELING, FOLLOW-UP SUPPORT	35 APARTMENTS FOR MEN, 4 BEDS FOR WOMEN, 10 TRANSITIONAL ROOMS; 661+ VETERANS SERVED SINCE 2010
EL-ADA COMMUNITY ACTION PARTNERSHIP	SUPPORTIVE SERVICES FOR VETERAN FAMILIES (SSVF), GPD BRIDGE HOUSING, CASE MANAGEMENT, FINANCIAL ASSISTANCE	174 VETERAN HOUSEHOLDS ASSISTED IN FISCAL YEAR 2024; 94 PERCENT EXIT TO PERMANENT HOUSING
CATCH (CHARITABLE ASSISTANCE TO COMMUNITY'S HOMELESS)	RAPID REHOUSING, FAMILY HOMELESSNESS PREVENTION, HOUSING NAVIGATION	TAKING ROOT PROGRAM EXPANDED TO 161 BEDS IN 2025
TERRY REILLY HEALTH SERVICES	HEALTH CARE FOR THE HOMELESS, INCLUDING VETERANS; BEHAVIORAL HEALTH, DENTAL, AND CASE MANAGEMENT	SERVES ADA AND CANYON COUNTIES
DISABLED AMERICAN VETERANS (DAV) OF IDAHO	TRANSPORTATION, BENEFITS NAVIGATION, VOCATIONAL REHABILITATION SUPPORT	VOLUNTEER DRIVER PROGRAM, ADVOCACY

Table 3: Key Nonprofit Providers for Homeless Veterans

These organizations often collaborate with the VA and local government, but also operate independent programs tailored to the unique needs of homeless veterans.

PROGRAM EFFECTIVENESS AND REACH

Boise Rescue Mission Ministries' VMP is notable for its long-term commitment to veterans, offering not only shelter and food but also individualized case management and ongoing follow-up after housing placement. The program's reported success rate—over 660 veterans transitioned to independence—demonstrates its impact, though capacity remains limited relative to need.

El-Ada's SSVF program boasts a 94 percent permanent housing exit rate for veteran households, reflecting the effectiveness of rapid rehousing and case management when adequately funded. CATCH's Taking Root program, supported by increased federal and private funding, has significantly expanded rapid rehousing capacity for families, including veteran households.

HOUSING ASSISTANCE: AVAILABILITY, TYPES, AND WAITLISTS

TYPES OF HOUSING ASSISTANCE

Homeless veterans in Boise have access to several forms of housing assistance, each with distinct eligibility criteria, funding sources, and service models.

PROGRAM TYPE	DESCRIPTION	CAPACITY WAITLIST
HUD-VASH (PERMANENT SUPPORTIVE HOUSING)	RENTAL ASSISTANCE VOUCHERS + CASE MANAGEMENT FOR CHRONICALLY HOMELESS VETERANS	CAPACITY VARIES; WAITLISTS POSSIBLE; MUST BE VA HEALTHCARE ELIGIBLE AND AGREE TO CASE MANAGEMENT
GRANT AND PER DIEM (GPD)	TRANSITIONAL HOUSING WITH SUPPORTIVE SERVICES (UP TO 24 MONTHS)	LIMITED BEDS; OFTEN AT CAPACITY
SUPPORTIVE SERVICES FOR VETERAN FAMILIES (SSVF)	RAPID REHOUSING AND HOMELESSNESS PREVENTION FOR VETERANS AND FAMILIES	174 HOUSEHOLDS SERVED BY EL-ADA IN FY2024; 94 PERCENT EXIT TO PERMANENT HOUSING
EMERGENCY SHELTER	IMMEDIATE, SHORT-TERM SHELTER (E.G., BOISE RESCUE MISSION)	35 APARTMENTS FOR MEN, 4 BEDS FOR WOMEN, 10 TRANSITIONAL ROOMS AT BRMM
TRANSITIONAL HOUSING	TIME-LIMITED, SERVICE-RICH HOUSING TO PREPARE FOR PERMANENT PLACEMENT	LIMITED; OFTEN INTEGRATED WITH GPD OR VMP
PERMANENT SUPPORTIVE HOUSING (NON-VA)	COMMUNITY-BASED HOUSING WITH INTENSIVE CASE MANAGEMENT	CAPACITY LIMITED BY FUNDING AND UNIT AVAILABILITY

Table 4: Housing Assistance Programs for Homeless Veterans

AVAILABILITY AND WAITLISTS

The availability of permanent supportive housing, especially HUD-VASH vouchers, is a critical determinant of housing outcomes for homeless veterans. The Boise City and Ada County Housing Authorities administer the HUD-VASH program in partnership with the Boise

VAMC, with eligibility determined by VA healthcare status and homelessness. Veterans must agree to ongoing case management as a condition of participation.

Waitlists for HUD-VASH and GPD programs fluctuate based on funding, voucher turnover, and local demand. During periods of high need, veterans may wait weeks or months for a voucher or bed to become available. The SSVF program, by contrast, is designed for rapid response and can often place eligible veterans into housing more quickly, though funding limitations can constrain reach.

Recent years have seen an expansion of rapid rehousing beds, particularly through CATCH's Taking Root program, which increased its capacity by 50 percent in 2025 (from 109 to 161 beds), including a focus on families fleeing domestic violence. However, the overall shortage of affordable housing in Boise—driven by rapid population growth, rising rents, and low vacancy rates—remains a structural barrier to ending veteran homelessness.

HOUSING MARKET CONTEXT

Idaho's population grew by 17.3 percent from 2010 to 2020, with housing values increasing nearly 75 percent from 2015 to 2020. The median home value in 2020 was $338,751, and 42.1 percent of renters were cost-burdened, paying more than 30 percent of their income on housing. These trends have intensified competition for affordable units, making it harder for veterans with limited income or rental histories to secure housing.

MENTAL HEALTH SERVICES FOR HOMELESS VETERANS

VA AND COMMUNITY PROVIDERS

Mental health care is a cornerstone of the VA Boise's offerings, with the Behavioral Health Department providing both inpatient and outpatient services, including telehealth appointments for rural veterans. Services include psychiatry, psychology, addiction treatment, and specialized care for PTSD, depression, and military sexual trauma.

The VA's mental health services are confidential and available to veterans, regardless of VA health care enrollment, for certain conditions. The Boise VAMC is recognized as a regional center of excellence for veteran-focused mental health care, and care coordinators are available to help veterans access appropriate treatment.

Community providers, such as Terry Reilly Health Services and Ada County-approved treatment centers, supplement VA services by offering counseling, crisis intervention, and ongoing therapy. These providers are particularly important for veterans who are ineligible for VA care or prefer non-VA settings.

ACCESS AND EFFECTIVENESS

Access to mental health care is generally good for veterans enrolled in VA health care, with telehealth options expanding reach to rural and mobility-limited veterans. However, recent and proposed federal staffing reductions have raised concerns about continuity of care and the capacity to meet growing demand. Community advocates and providers have protested budget cuts, warning that Idaho's already limited behavioral health infrastructure cannot absorb additional demand if VA services are reduced.

Military veterans are 57.3 percent more likely to die by suicide than non-veteran US adults, underscoring the critical importance of accessible, high-quality mental health care. Continuity of care, including consistent follow-ups with trusted providers, is a key factor in suicide prevention and recovery.

For veterans unable to access VA mental health services, safety net options such as Idaho's free and charitable clinics provide essential care, though these resources are limited and often stretched thin.

SUBSTANCE USE TREATMENT ACCESS FOR VETERANS

VA AND COMMUNITY-BASED TREATMENT

The Boise VAMC offers comprehensive substance abuse treatment programs tailored to veterans, including residential inpatient, outpatient, and detoxification services. Treatment approaches include evidence-based therapies such as cognitive behavioral therapy (CBT), dialectical behavior therapy (DBT), trauma-informed counseling, and medication-assisted treatment (MAT) for opioid and alcohol use disorders.

The VA's Substance Abuse Residential Rehabilitation Treatment Program (SARRTP) provides 24/7 medical supervision and intensive treatment for veterans in crisis or with acute needs. The program emphasizes holistic care, addressing both substance use and co-occurring mental health disorders, and supports reintegration into the community.

Community providers, including Ada County-approved treatment centers and organizations like Port of Hope and Raise the Bottom, offer outpatient, intensive outpatient, and residential treatment options. These programs accept a range of payment sources, including Medicaid, Medicare, private insurance, and federal funding.

BARRIERS AND GAPS

While the VA offers a robust CoC, barriers to access persist. These include:

- **Eligibility:** Veterans with less-than-honorable discharges may be ineligible for VA-funded treatment.

- **Capacity:** Limited residential and detoxification beds can result in waitlists, particularly during surges in demand.

- **Transportation:** Reaching treatment facilities can be challenging for veterans without reliable transportation, especially those living outside central Boise.

- **Stigma:** Some veterans are reluctant to seek help due to stigma associated with addiction or mental health issues.

Community providers help fill these gaps, but coordination between VA and non-VA programs is essential to ensure seamless transitions and avoid service duplication.

EMPLOYMENT AND VOCATIONAL SUPPORT FOR HOMELESS VETERANS

VETERAN READINESS AND EMPLOYMENT (VR&E)

The VA's VR&E program, formerly known as Vocational Rehabilitation and Employment, is designed to help veterans with service-connected disabilities prepare for, find, and maintain suitable employment. Eligibility requires a service-connected disability rating of at least 10 percent and a demonstrated job handicap. Services include career counseling, education and training, job-search assistance, resume building, interview preparation, and support for self-employment.

Veterans can access VR&E services by applying for VA disability benefits, obtaining a letter of eligibility, and working with a counselor to develop an individualized employment plan. The Boise VA Regional Benefit Office provides in-person and virtual appointments for benefits navigation and vocational support.

HOMELESS VETERANS' REINTEGRATION PROGRAM (HVRP)

The US Department of Labor's HVRP provides employment and training services to homeless veterans, including those at risk of homelessness or recently released from incarceration. HVRP grantees offer job readiness training, placement assistance, and supportive services to help veterans achieve economic self-sufficiency.

LOCAL AND NONPROFIT INITIATIVES

Nonprofit organizations, such as the Boise Rescue Mission Ministries and DAV of Idaho, offer job training, life skills development, and employment support as part of their broader veterans' programs. These services are often integrated with housing and case management to address the multiple barriers faced by homeless veterans.

OUTCOMES AND CHALLENGES

Employment support is a critical component of long-term stability for formerly homeless veterans. However, barriers such as lack of identification, criminal records, gaps in employment history, and ongoing health issues can impede job placement. Coordination between VA, Department of Labor programs, and local nonprofits is essential to provide comprehensive, individualized support.

VA BENEFITS NAVIGATION AND REGIONAL BENEFIT OFFICE SERVICES

BOISE VA REGIONAL BENEFIT OFFICE

The Boise VA Regional Benefit Office assists veterans, service members, and their families in accessing VA benefits, including disability compensation, education benefits, pensions, life insurance, and home loans. The office offers walk-in and appointment-based services, with virtual appointments available through the Visitor Engagement Reporting Application (VERA).

Benefit counselors guide veterans through eligibility determination, document gathering, application completion, and claim status tracking. The office also provides support for family members and caregivers, survivor benefits, and transition assistance for service members leaving the military.

BARRIERS TO BENEFITS ACCESS

Navigating the VA benefits system can be daunting, especially for homeless veterans who may lack necessary documentation (e.g., DD214, identification), have complex medical histories, or face cognitive or mental health challenges. The Boise VA Regional Benefit Office works to streamline access, but some veterans require intensive case management or legal assistance to resolve eligibility issues.

Nonprofit organizations and accredited representatives, such as DAV of Idaho, play a vital role in helping veterans understand their rights, complete applications, and appeal denials.

BARRIERS TO ACCESS: TRANSPORTATION, ELIGIBILITY, AWARENESS, AND STIGMA

TRANSPORTATION

Transportation is a significant barrier for homeless veterans in Boise, particularly those living in outlying areas or with mobility limitations. While the VA and local nonprofits offer some transportation assistance, gaps remain.

SERVICE OR PROVIDER	DESCRIPTION	ELIGIBILITY AND NOTES
DAV OF IDAHO TRANSPORTATION	FREE SHUTTLE SERVICES TO VA MEDICAL CENTERS, COORDINATED RIDES FOR ESSENTIAL SERVICES	REQUEST VIA DAV WEBSITE; VOLUNTEER-DRIVEN
VALLEY REGIONAL TRANSIT (VRT)	FIXED-ROUTE BUSES, PARATRANSIT, BEYOND ACCESS (DOOR-TO-DOOR FOR SENIORS AND VETERANS), MERIDIAN VETERANS SHUTTLE	REDUCED FARES FOR VETERANS; COVERAGE VARIES
RIDES2WELLNESS	FREE TRANSPORTATION TO MEDICAL APPOINTMENTS FOR PATIENTS OF ST. LUKE'S, SAINT ALPHONSUS, AND DESIGNATED CLINICS	MUST BE A PATIENT AT PARTICIPATING CLINICS
VOLUNTEER DRIVER PROGRAMS	PERSONALIZED RIDES FOR MEDICAL AND SOCIAL SERVICE APPOINTMENTS	SCHEDULE THROUGH DAV OR LOCAL PROVIDERS

Table 5: Transportation Services for Boise Veterans

Despite these options, veterans may face challenges such as limited service hours, the need for advance scheduling, and limited coverage in rural or suburban areas.

ELIGIBILITY

Eligibility criteria for VA and community programs can exclude some veterans, particularly those with less-than-honorable discharges, insufficient service duration, or lack of documentation. The definition of "veteran" varies by program, and some services require proof of homelessness or income verification.

AWARENESS AND NAVIGATION

Many homeless veterans are unaware of available resources or struggle to navigate the complex web of services. Outreach and case management are essential to connect veterans with appropriate supports. The use of navigators—dedicated staff who guide veterans through the system—has been identified as a best practice for improving access and outcomes.

STIGMA

Stigma associated with homelessness, mental illness, and substance use can deter veterans from seeking help. Peer support, trauma-informed care, and culturally competent services are important for reducing stigma and building trust.

RECENT INITIATIVES, POLICY CHANGES, AND FUNDING

FEDERAL AND LOCAL POLICY DEVELOPMENTS

Recent years have seen both expansions and threats to veterans' services in Boise. Increased federal funding has enabled the expansion of rapid rehousing and supportive housing programs, such as CATCH's Taking Root initiative. However, proposed and actual cuts to the VA's budget and workforce have raised concerns about the sustainability of core services.

In 2025, the US Department of Veterans Affairs backed away from plans for mass layoffs but still anticipates reducing its nationwide workforce by 30,000, with approximately 300 jobs at risk at the Boise facility. Community protests and advocacy have highlighted the potential impact on mental health and behavioral health services, which are already stretched thin in Idaho.

On the positive side, the reauthorization of VA's authority to provide food, water, and essential goods through fiscal year 2027, and the permanent authorization for telehealth services, have improved access for low-income and rural veterans.

LOCAL INITIATIVES

The City of Boise and Ada County have invested in data transparency and service coordination through the Housing Data Portal and Our Path Home partnership. The expansion of rapid rehousing beds and targeted funding for family homelessness has improved outcomes for some subpopulations.

The VA's "unsheltered surge" initiatives, modeled after successful efforts in other cities, have focused on proactive outreach, same-day access to interim housing, and coordinated transitions to permanent housing.

COORDINATION AND GAPS BETWEEN VA AND COMMUNITY PROVIDERS

COLLABORATION MODELS

Effective service delivery for homeless veterans in Boise depends on strong coordination between the VA, local government, and nonprofit providers. The CoC model, led by Our Path Home, brings together more than forty agencies to make homelessness rare, brief, and non-recurring.

Best practices identified in national and local reports include:

- **Community-wide Lists:** Creating and sharing a master list of homeless veterans across agencies to prioritize resources and avoid duplication.
- **Standardized Assessments:** Using tools like the VI-SPDAT to triage and target interventions based on vulnerability and need.
- **Navigators:** Assigning dedicated staff to guide veterans through the housing and service system until stable housing is achieved.
- **Regular Case Conferencing:** Interagency meetings to review cases, coordinate care, and resolve barriers.

PERSISTENT GAPS

Despite these efforts, gaps remain in communication, data sharing, and resource allocation. Privacy concerns and incompatible data systems can impede information sharing. Some veterans fall through the cracks due to eligibility issues, lack of engagement, or complex needs that exceed the capacity of existing programs.

TRANSPORTATION AND GEOGRAPHIC REACH

PUBLIC AND SPECIALIZED TRANSPORTATION

Boise's public transportation system, operated by VRT, offers fixed-route buses, paratransit, and specialized services for veterans and seniors. The Meridian Veterans Shuttle provides service between Meridian and the Boise VA hospital, while the Beyond Access program offers door-to-door rides for eligible individuals.

The DAV of Idaho's volunteer driver program supplements public transit by providing free rides to medical appointments and essential services. However, service hours, coverage areas, and the need for advance scheduling can limit accessibility, especially for veterans living outside the urban core or with urgent needs.

GEOGRAPHIC BARRIERS

Boise's rapid growth and suburban expansion have increased the distance between affordable housing, services, and employment opportunities. Veterans living in outlying areas may face long commutes or limited transportation options, exacerbating isolation and hindering access to care.

DATA SOURCES AND METRICS

POINT-IN-TIME (PIT) AND HOUSING INVENTORY COUNT (HIC)

The annual PIT Count, conducted each January, provides a snapshot of homelessness in Ada County, including the number of veterans experiencing homelessness. The 2025 PIT Count found 772 individuals experiencing homelessness, with a small decrease from the previous year.

The HIC, conducted simultaneously, tracks the number and types of beds dedicated to people experiencing homelessness, including veterans. In 2025, rapid rehousing beds increased significantly, driven by CATCH's Taking Root program.

LOCAL DASHBOARDS AND STATEWIDE ANALYSIS

The City of Boise's Housing Data Portal and the Idaho Policy Institute's Statewide Housing Analysis offer detailed data on housing needs, affordability, and cost burden across the region. The House Idaho Collaborative maintains a community dashboard tracking service utilization and outcomes.

NATIONAL REPORTS

The Annual Homelessness Assessment Report (AHAR) to Congress and VA's Homeless Programs Office white papers provide national and regional context, highlighting trends, best practices, and policy recommendations.

OUTCOMES AND EFFECTIVENESS

HOUSING RETENTION

Programs such as El-Ada's SSVF report a 94 percent permanent housing exit rate for veteran households, indicating strong effectiveness when adequate resources and case management are available. The Boise Rescue Mission Ministries' VMP has transitioned over 660 veterans to independence since 2010, with ongoing follow-up support to promote housing stability.

TREATMENT OUTCOMES

The Boise VA Medical Center's integrated approach to mental health and substance use treatment, including evidence-based therapies and medication-assisted treatment, supports recovery and resilience. However, outcome data specific to Boise is limited, and ongoing evaluation is needed to assess long-term impacts.

EMPLOYMENT

Employment outcomes for homeless veterans are mixed, with barriers such as disabilities, criminal records, and gaps in work history impeding job placement. The VR&E and HVRP programs provide critical support, but comprehensive, individualized assistance is required for sustained success.

COMMUNITY PERCEPTIONS, ADVOCACY, AND MEDIA COVERAGE

ADVOCACY AND PUBLIC AWARENESS

Community advocacy has played a significant role in shaping the response to veteran homelessness in Boise. Protests and media coverage have highlighted the risks posed by federal budget cuts and staffing reductions at the VA, galvanizing support for preserving and expanding essential services.

Public-private partnerships, such as Our Path Home, have fostered a sense of shared responsibility and collective action. Media coverage of program successes, such as the expansion of rapid rehousing beds and the achievements of the Veterans Ministry Program, has helped raise awareness and reduce stigma.

LEGAL AND ELIGIBILITY ISSUES

DISCHARGE STATUS AND DOCUMENTATION

Eligibility for VA services depends on discharge status; those discharged under conditions other than dishonorable are generally eligible for most programs. However, some veterans with less-than-honorable discharges are excluded from VA-funded housing and health care, though community providers may serve them.

Lack of documentation, such as a DD214 or government-issued ID, can impede access to benefits, housing, and employment. Programs such as the Boise VA Regional Benefit Office and nonprofit navigators assist veterans in obtaining necessary documents, but the process can be lengthy and complex.

CRIMINAL RECORDS

Veterans with criminal records, particularly those recently released from incarceration, face additional barriers to housing and employment. The HVRP program and some local initiatives specifically target this population, offering reintegration support and advocacy.

BEST PRACTICES AND MODELS FROM COMPARABLE CITIES

NATIONAL AND REGIONAL INNOVATIONS

Best practices identified in national reports and implemented in Boise include:

- **Low-Barrier, Trauma-Informed Care:** Reducing documentation and eligibility requirements to facilitate rapid access to shelter and services.
- **Co-Location of Services:** Bringing VA, benefits, and housing staff together for same-day enrollment and coordinated care.
- **Permanent Housing Surges:** Proactively moving veterans from interim to permanent housing to free up beds for unsheltered veterans.
- **Regular Case Conferencing:** Interagency meetings to review cases and coordinate interventions.
- **Navigator Programs:** Assigning dedicated staff to guide veterans through the system until stable housing is achieved.

Cities such as Denver and Fresno have demonstrated the effectiveness of these approaches, and Boise has adopted similar models through its One Team coordination and surge initiatives.

RESOURCE MAPPING AND SERVICE DIRECTORY

PROVIDER OR PROGRAM	SERVICE TYPE	CONTACT AND LOCATION
VA BOISE MEDICAL CENTER	HEALTH, MENTAL HEALTH, SUBSTANCE USE, HOUSING	500 W. FORT ST., BOISE, ID; (208) 422-1000
VA REGIONAL BENEFIT OFFICE	BENEFITS NAVIGATION, EMPLOYMENT SUPPORT	444 W. FORT ST., BOISE, ID; (208) 429-2228
BOISE RESCUE MISSION MINISTRIES	TRANSITIONAL HOUSING, CASE MANAGEMENT, FOOD, COUNSELING	PO BOX 1494, BOISE, ID; (208) 343-2389
EL-ADA COMMUNITY ACTION PARTNERSHIP	SSVF, GPD BRIDGE HOUSING, CASE MANAGEMENT	2250 S. VISTA AVE., BOISE, ID; (208) 345-2820
CATCH	RAPID REHOUSING, FAMILY HOMELESSNESS PREVENTION	WWW.CATCHPROGRAM.ORG
TERRY REILLY HEALTH SERVICES	HEALTH CARE, BEHAVIORAL HEALTH, DENTAL, CASE MANAGEMENT	300 S. 23RD ST., BOISE, ID; (208) 345-1170
DAV OF IDAHO	TRANSPORTATION, BENEFITS NAVIGATION, ADVOCACY	WWW.DAV-IDAHO.ORG
VRT	PUBLIC TRANSPORTATION, PARATRANSIT, VETERANS SHUTTLE	WWW.VALLEYREGIONALTRANSIT.ORG
ADA COUNTY-APPROVED PROVIDERS	SUBSTANCE USE AND MENTAL HEALTH TREATMENT	SEE COUNTY PROVIDER LIST

Table 6: Directory of Key Providers and Services for Homeless Veterans in Boise

This directory is not exhaustive but highlights the primary access points for homeless veterans seeking assistance in Boise.

CONCLUSION AND RECOMMENDATIONS

The accessibility of veterans' resources for the homeless population in Boise, Idaho, is shaped by a complex interplay of federal, state, local, and nonprofit programs. While the VA and its partners offer a comprehensive array of services—including housing assistance, mental health care, substance use treatment, employment support, and benefits navigation—barriers such as limited capacity, eligibility restrictions, transportation challenges, and systemic fragmentation persist.

Key strengths of Boise's system include strong nonprofit engagement, effective rapid rehousing and case management models, and a commitment to data-driven coordination through the CoC. **Persistent challenges** include the shortage of affordable housing, the impact of federal staffing reductions, and the need for improved outreach and navigation for the most vulnerable veterans.

Recommendations for enhancing accessibility and effectiveness include:

1. **Expand low-barrier, trauma-informed access** to shelter and services, minimizing documentation and eligibility hurdles.

2. **Increase permanent supportive housing capacity** through additional HUD-VASH vouchers and local partnerships.

3. **Strengthen transportation networks** for veterans, especially those in outlying areas or with mobility limitations.

4. **Enhance outreach and navigation**, employing dedicated navigators and peer support to connect veterans with resources.

5. **Foster interagency collaboration and data sharing**, leveraging best practices from comparable cities and national models.

6. **Advocate for sustained and increased funding** at the federal and local levels to preserve and expand critical services.

7. **Address legal and eligibility barriers**, including support for veterans with less-than-honorable discharges and those lacking documentation.

8. **Monitor and evaluate outcomes**, using local dashboards and national benchmarks to guide continuous improvement.

By building on existing strengths and addressing persistent gaps, Boise can continue to make progress toward the goal of ending veteran homelessness and ensuring that all who have served have access to the support and dignity they deserve.

References

Boise City/Ada County HMIS. "BCAC Point In Time Count Dashboard." Created by the Institute for Community Alliances. Accessed March 30, 2026. https://public.tableau.com/app/profile/boise.city.ada.county.hmis/viz/BCACPointInTimeCountDashboard/PITOverview.

Boise Rescue Mission Ministries. "Veterans." Accessed March 30, 2026. https://boiserm.org/services/veterans/.

Boise Rescue Mission Ministries. *Veterans Ministry Program*. Brochure. Boise, ID, October 2025. https://boiserm.org/wp-content/uploads/2025/10/2025-10-Veterans-Ministry-Program-Trifold-Final.pdf.

CATCH. "Taking Root." Accessed March 30, 2026. https://catchidaho.org/taking-root/.

City of Boise. "Our Path Home Shares 2025 Point-In-Time Count Results." September 29, 2025. https://www.cityofboise.org/news/planning-and-development-services/2025/september/our-path-home-shares-2025-point-in-time-count-results/.

Crossgrove Fry, Vanessa, Lantz McGinnis-Brown, Cheong Kim, and Matthew May. Idaho Statewide Housing Analysis 2022. Boise, ID: Boise State University, 2022. https://scholarworks.boisestate.edu/ipi_reports/60/

Disabled American Veterans, Department of Idaho. "Become a Volunteer Driver for DAV of Idaho." Accessed March 30, 2026. https://dav-idaho.org/become-a-driver/.

El-Ada Community Action Partnership. "Veteran Services." Accessed March 30, 2026. https://www.eladacap.org/veteran-services.

National Health Care for the Homeless Council. "Terry Reilly Health Services." Accessed March 30, 2026. https://nhchc.org/terry-reilly-health-services/.

Our Path Home. *2025 ADA County Point-in-Time Count*. Infographic. Accessed March 30, 2026. https://www.ourpathhome.org/media/1204/oph_pit_2025_infographic.pdf.

Terry Reilly Health Services. Accessed March 30, 2026. https://www.trhs.org/.

U.S. Department of Veterans Affairs, Office of Mental Health and Suicide Prevention. *Ways Veterans Differ from the General Population*. Fact Sheet. January 2022. https://www.mentalhealth.va.gov/suicide_prevention/docs/FSTP-Ways-Veterans-Differ-from-the-General-Population.pdf.

U.S. Department of Veterans Affairs, Office of Mental Health and Suicide Prevention. *2022 National Veteran Suicide Prevention Annual Report*. September 2022. https://www.mentalhealth.va.gov/docs/data-sheets/2022/2022-National-Veteran-Suicide-Prevention-Annual-Report-FINAL-508.pdf.

Acknowledgments

No one rebuilds alone. I owe deep gratitude to everyone who walked beside me, lifted me when I couldn't stand, and showed me how to pass the help forward.

To the VA's Veterans Justice Outreach (VJO) Program—you reached into that jail cell darkness and pulled me toward light. Your persistence saved my life. To my family, who saw me at my worst and still believed there was something worth saving, thank you for your patience, your prayers, and your presence.

To the Boise Rescue Mission Ministries—Rev. Bill Roscoe and the entire team at the River of Life shelter—you gave me more than shelter; you gave me structure, dignity, and a path forward. The New Life Program was not just recovery; it was rebirth.

Finally, to every veteran I have crossed paths with on my journey—you are too numerous to name, but your impact is immeasurable. Thank you.

About the Author

Don Lineberry is a U.S. Army veteran who served as an M60A1 tank gunner in Germany during the Cold War era, followed by service in the Idaho National Guard's 116th Armored Cavalry. Now based in Nampa, Idaho (near Boise), he serves as senior case manager in the Boise Rescue Mission Ministries' Veterans Ministry Program, where he helps other veterans experiencing homelessness and addiction through the same year-long, faith-based New Life Program from which he graduated in 2016. He also advocates in Veterans Treatment Court and is the director of his local American Legion Riders chapter (Post 113 in the Treasure Valley area), organizing rides, events like Patriot Thunder, and community service focused on veteran support, patriotism, and charity.

By sharing his story, he hopes to raise awareness about ordinary veteran pain (invisible wounds leading to addiction/isolation), extraordinary mercy (VJO, faith-based recovery, community support), and ongoing service. His lived experiences are not unique, but proof that *collapse isn't the end* and *the rise is coming* through persistence, honesty, and help. He positions the book as a resource and a lantern for others who feel forgotten or too far gone, especially veterans. Meanwhile, his work continues to focus on veteran outreach and recovery support.

For more, visit riverbottomsbook.com (his author site) or boiserm.org (Mission site, where he works).